MW00718601

The Tom Tyler Story

From Cowboy Star
to Super Hero

Also by Mike Chapman

Two Guys Named Dan
Kings of the Mat
Toughest Men in Sports
Evy and the Hawkeyes (co-author)
Gotch To Gable: A History of Iowa Wrestling
Iowans of Impact
The New Breed: Living Iowa Wrestling (co-author)
Nick and The Cyclones
Gotch: World's Greatest Wrestler
Encyclopedia of American Wrestling
Fighting Back
Gotch: An American Hero
Please Don't Call Me Tarzan
The Gold and The Glory
Lowell Park
Achilles: Son of Peleus, Scourge of Troy
Wrestling Tough

The Tom Tyler Story

From Cowboy Star
to Super Hero

By

Mike Chapman

With Bobby Copeland

CULTURE HOUSE BOOKS

The Tom Tyler Story, From Cowboy Star to Super Hero

A Culture House Book / June 2005
All Rights Reserved

For information, address: Culture House Books
                              P.O. Box 293
                              Newton, Iowa 50208

Library of Congress Cataloging-in-Publication Data
Chapman, Mike, 1943 -
    The Tom Tyler Story, From Cowboy Star to Super Hero / Mike Chapman
    1. Tyler, Tom   2. Cowboy movie star   3. Captain Marvel   4. The Phantom
    5. Movie history   6. Weightlifting history

ISBN# 0-9676080-8-2

PRINTED IN THE UNITED STATES of AMERICA

First Edition

Front Cover Photo: "Trigger Tom," Reliable/Steiner.
Captain Marvel is a trademark character of DC Comics.
The Phantom is a trademark character of King Features Syndicate.

*Worldly fame is but a breath of wind
that blows this way, and now that,
and changes names as it changes directions.*

– Dante

Acknowledgements

This book is the result of many years of "on-and-off" research, and several months of rather intense probing. While searching for the real Tom Tyler, I traveled to Hamtramck, Michigan; to Victorville, California, and to Hollywood. I corresponded with a variety of people, foremost among who were Bobby Copeland, Ray Slepski and Mike Tyler. Bobby is one of the nation's foremost western film historians. He offered important assistance and helped provide historical perspective.

Ray Slepski and Mike Tyler are nephews of Tom Tyler and offered important insights into the life of Tom, and into the nature of his family relations. They also provided most of the personal photos used in the book. Their wives, Joanne Slepski and Harriet Tyler, were very helpful, as well. I am also indebted to the following people for their assistance along the way: Chuck Anderson, Calvin Castine, Boyd Magers, Thomas Karkoski, Brian Walker, Marilyn Beaudrie, Tony and Susan Redge, Carl Mastromarino and Kim Beckwith, who did considerable research at the University of Texas on Tom's weightlifting exploits. I found some interesting tidbits about Tom and his film career at the beautiful Margaret Herrick Library in Beverly Hills. I also appreciate the assistance of Jacqueline Blint, education manager of the Scleroderma Foundation in Byfield, Massachusetts, in helping me understand that terrible disease.

As always, I received tremendous support from my wife of many years, Beverly. One of the most poignant moments of my work on this book was to see Bev and Joanne Slepski, the wife of Ray Slepski, kneeling side by side to clean the area around the gravestone of Tom Tyler in the Mt. Olivet Cemetery in Hamtramck. I can only imagine that somewhere, somehow, Vincent Markowski was smiling down at these two lovely ladies on that sunlit afternoon in the town where his grand desire took root and blossomed.

Table of Contents

Introduction

From the moment when I first decided to write a biography of Tom Tyler, I knew it was a daunting chore that lay ahead of me. I had done enough research through the years to realize there was a real scarcity of material about the great B western and serial film star of the 1920s, '30s and '40s, and I had talked to several western film buffs that said the assignment would be very difficult.

"It's great to hear that you're working on a bio of Tom Tyler," wrote one authority on old-time movies, "but I don't envy you the task. Finding information about him, whether personal or career-related, is like pulling teeth. Nearly everyone he worked with is deceased. Worse still is that he didn't get a lot of ink in the press even during the height of his career."

His words turned out to be prophetic. Though the "reel" Tom Tyler was ubiquitous, the "real" Tom Tyler is nearly anonymous to most of his fans, who still exist more than half a century after he passed from the scene. And he is certainly a mysterious figure to anyone who hopes to learn more about him by delving into his past.

Tyler was not a superstar in the Hollywood pantheon, but he was a very successful actor on several levels. He was a well-known cowboy B star for nearly three decades and appeared in some of the most memorable films ever made, such as "Gone With the Wind" and "Stagecoach." In addition, he played the lead in several very successful serials, including "The Adventures of Captain Marvel" and "The Phantom."

Extremely handsome and athletic, he looked the part of a western star as much as any actor who ever rode across the silver screen, including the more popular Tom Mix and Buck Jones. And yet, remarkably, very little is known about Tyler's life apart from his work. He was born in a small hamlet in New York, moved to the Detroit area with his family when in his early teens, headed for Hollywood at age twenty, was a sensational weightlifter, married once (for a brief time), and died at age fifty, of a rare and devastating illness. Beyond that, there is not much information to be found about the man.

Still, I wanted to try and tell his story, as best I could from the scant evidence available. The primary reasons were simple, really: Tom Tyler was one of the most productive and attractive actors in Hollywood history, and what little I did know of him inspired me to try and learn more. I had always admired the cowboy B stars that I watched on television in the 1950s as a youth in my home in Waterloo, Iowa, and I loved the comic-book characters Captain Marvel and the Phantom.

Being a longtime weight trainer myself, I grew even more intrigued with Tyler's life when I learned that he was an outstanding weightlifter. Then when I read about the disease that hastened the end of his life, I was hooked. Scleroderma seemed like such a horrible condition that I wanted to know more about it and, hence, more about Tom Tyler.

One of my first efforts in tracing the life of this enigmatic star was to begin searching the Internet for clues. That's how I happened across Bobby Copeland, who has written several books about other western film stars and knew far more about that genre than I did. He was immediately attracted to the project and we decided to pool our resources and talents to come up with this book. I did the traveling and the writing while Bobby offered information on who to contact and helped acquire background information on Tyler, his movie credits, and the era of the B cowboy stars.

Then I made contact with several surviving members of the extended family of Tom Tyler. I exchanged emails with Marilyn Beaudrie, whose sister Joanne married Ray Slepski, Tom Tyler's nephew and godson. In September of 2004, I met with Marilyn, Ray and Joanne, as well as nephew Tom Kozyra and his wife, Betty, and nephew Tony Redge, and his wife, Susie, in Detroit. Ray and Joanne then gave my wife and me a wonderful tour of the old Hamtramck neighborhood where the Markowski family moved into when Tom was still a teenager. We drove by the house on Mitchell Street where Tom lived prior to leaving for Hollywood and then to the house on Moenart, where Ray was raised and Tom Tyler came back to for his final years. We even met with the current owners of the house and were invited inside; it was a very nostalgic tour for Ray and Joanne, bringing back wonderful memories of the Slepski family and of Tom Tyler's final sad months.

Later, I talked with Sandy Slepski, Ray's sister and Tom Tyler's niece, who helped me make contact with Mike and Harriet Tyler. Mike and Harriet are retired and live in Victorville, California. They have a marvelous collection of Tom Tyler memorabilia, including a huge oil painting, dozens of original movie posters from the 1930s, and literally hundreds of lobby cards, pressbooks and photos. I am deeply indebted to all of the Tyler relatives for sharing with me all they know and remember of their Uncle Tom. What came shining through in my conversations with them is the tremendous admiration they all hold for Tom Tyler, both as a man and for his remarkable film career.

This project is the result of my forty years of interest in the life and times of Tom Tyler. I hope you will enjoy reading it as much as I enjoyed researching it, and that you, too, will come to appreciate the life of this very intriguing person.

Mike Chapman
Newton, Iowa

Tom Tyler at age 21

The Old Man Down the Street

The curious boys and girls living in the old Polish section of Detroit near Moenart Street surely noticed the "old man" who lived at the attractive three-story brick home at 13158. Some time in the winter of 1952-53, he had moved into the house owned by the Leonard and Katherine Slepski family. The neighborhood kids had most likely seen him sitting on his chair on the front porch or moving slowly down the street, and gave him little more than a curious glance. But a year after his arrival, they would know much more about him and would be eager to pay their respects.

Though he was physically hampered and appeared older than his fifty years, the newcomer was a rare breed of man. Just twenty years earlier, he had been one of the most physically attractive actors in all of Hollywood... lean and muscular, tall and handsome. Though not a major star on the level with a Douglas Fairbanks or a Clark Gable, he was nonetheless an integral player in the world of the B westerns, and in the popular serials that excited young moviegoers all around the world. He even had roles in two of the most popular films of all time, "Gone With the Wind" and "Stagecoach."

He not only was the star of nearly seventy western films he also played two of the grandest fictional characters in the entire world. Incredibly, he was both Captain Marvel and the Phantom of film. But in 1953, those days were long gone. By then, he was living in his sister's home in Detroit, wracked by a crippling disease and left with little more than fading memories of a once proud career. What they were seeing was the mere shadow of Tom Tyler as the final curtain was descending on his stage. It came down for the last time on May 3, 1954. When it did, word had slipped out that the man who had moved into the stately house on Moenart Street was an unusual person. Very unusual, indeed.

"Young and old Detroit paid tribute today to Tom Tyler, a Hamtramck factory worker who became one of Hollywood's first cowboy stars," began a story by Harry Salsinger in the May 4, 1954 edition of the Detroit News. "Living here virtually unknown, Tyler died Sunday after a heart attack.

"Although age and illness long had dragged him from the top ranks of the screen's western heroes, television has made a new hero of Tyler for a younger generation. Youngsters are now seeing the pictures that made his name famous to their parents.

"At the Wysocki Funeral Home, 5227 McNichols East, a legion of youngsters filed past his casket during the noon recess and after the final school bell this week.

"Tyler, who was born Vincent Markowski in Witherbee, N.Y., was brought here by his factory worker father when he was fifteen years old.

"Young Vincent, already a strapping, handsome boy, went to work in a factory too – but not for long. His family recalls that he always wanted to be an actor and, after six months in a shop, he ran away from home and worked his way west.

"Stardom wasn't waiting for Tyler when he arrived. He spent seven years waiting for his big chance. Fame came in a rush in 1927 (sic) when he was picked to star in 'Let's Go

Gallagher,' for FBO Pictures.

"From that moment on, Tyler was high in the Hollywood parade.

"Aging and periodically crippled by arthritis, Tyler gradually dropped out of his starring roles. He was most recently seen as a trooper in 'She Wore a Yellow Ribbon.'

"Television proved a boon for Tyler, who played not as star but as a heavy, in filmed TV shows. Ill health finally forced him to retire and, in November, 1952, he came here to live with his sister, Mrs. Katherine Slepski, at 13158 Moenart. Mrs. Slepski said he had planned to return to Hollywood next fall."

Services for Tom Tyler were held in St. Augustine Church and burial was in Mt. Olivet Cemetery.

Salsinger's story merely showed the tip of the iceberg in a remarkable life. It did not mention Tyler's showing in three very popular serials. Nor did it mention his sensational weightlifting career and the fact that he was a national champion in that sport and qualified to compete in the 1928 Olympics.

There is, however, much, much more to tell. When Vincent Markowski rode into Hollywood as a very young man in the mid-1920s, the film capital was still in its formative years. By the time he left nearly thirty years later, the world he knew had changed dramatically.

The Tom Tyler saga is a tremendous story – that of a blossoming industry that would some day hold the entire world in its palm, and of a young actor who struggled indefatigably to earn a place in that industry. It is a story worth telling and worth preserving.

The Cowboy Era

It was William S. Hart and Tom Mix who laid the foundation for the hugely-popular western film genre that existed for nearly half a century, and thereby set the stage for the creation of the man who would become known as Tom Tyler.

The western film era began innocently enough in 1903 when Edwin S. Porter, working for Thomas Edison's company, produced a little film entitled "The Great Train Robbery," featuring a fellow by the name of Broncho Billy Anderson. It was the start of a long career for Broncho Billy, who cranked out hundreds of more short thrillers. His work paved the way for the two most influential cowboy film stars of all time, Hart and Mix, who followed a dozen or more years later. Hart and Mix were as far apart as could be both on and off the screen, but they are forever united in the impact they had on Western film history. Ironically, they both came from the East.

Born on December 6, 1870, Hart was raised in rural New York. He traveled in the West as a boy with his father and developed a passion for the lore of the Native American and cowboy way of life that would define him all of his life. Back in New York, he turned to the stage as a young man and learned the acting craft well. He showed up in Hollywood in 1914 and, at the age of forty-four, became a box-office sensation as a western film actor. Hart had an appearance that was both noble and raw. A man of craggy features, he stressed simple cowboy attire and realism on the screen. He was determined to portray the West as he felt it really was, based on first-hand observation, and he directed most of his own films. He made 70-some films in a decade, between 1915 and 1925, and almost single-handedly shaped the new genre.

"Travelin' On (1920) was perhaps the last of what one may term vintage Hart films; already there were unmistakable signs that Hart's reign was almost over and that the public opinion had shifted in favor of the more colorful and more streamlined Tom Mix," wrote the authors of the book, *The Westerns; From Silents to Cinerama. (1)*

Mix was born in 1880, ten years after Hart, in a small village in rural Pennsylvania. He came to Hollywood in a roundabout way, holding various jobs in Oklahoma and other western states. He began in films as a rugged extra, ready to try any stunt on horseback. He soon parlayed his engaging personality and flamboyant style into the lead roles for the Selig Company and made a strong impact... strong enough that in 1917 William J. Fox hired him away to work at his much larger studio.

At Fox Studios, Mix began cranking out exciting westerns with fairly good budgets. They were gobbled up by an adoring public and Mix became a sensation all around the world. At his peak, he was considered on the same playing field with Charlie Chaplin, Douglas Fairbanks and Rudolph Valentino in terms of star power. He was mobbed at personal appearances and lived in a gaudy mansion in the Hollywood Hills. By 1925, he was making almost $20,000 a week and living like an emperor.

It is estimated that Mix appeared in nearly 200 films overall, counting both two-reelers and feature films. He also made the transition, albeit a bit rocky, from the silent era to the sound era.

"His films for Fox over a ten-year period literally made the company, just as the Autry Westerns in the mid-Thirties put Republic on the map," added the authors of *The Westerns; From Silents to Cinerama.* "Fox openly admitted Mix's value, giving him the full star treatment. The cowboy had his own production unit, an elaborate private bungalow – everything that went with the status of a Hollywood star in the movies' most colorful era." *(2)*

The successes of Hart and Mix opened the ranch gates to a long parade of cowboy film stars, of all sorts. As a group, they made a huge impression on youth all over America. Their exciting adventures and irrepressible personas nurtured the dreams of millions of young, red-blooded American boys from coast to coast – including a young boy in Dixon, Illinois, who was destined to become the fortieth President of the United States.

"There was the life that shaped my body and mind for all the years to come after," wrote Ronald Reagan in his autobiography. "Sitting in the Family Theatre watching the marvelous flickering antics of Tom Mix and William S. Hart as they foiled robbers and villains and escorted the beautiful girls to safety, waving back from their horses as they cantered into the sunset…." *(3)*

Also influenced by the Great Dream of Hollywood was a young Michigan teenager named Vincent Markowski, who was growing to maturity at the same time the movie industry was flexing its muscles. Like countless others, he was fascinated by the images that appeared on the giant screens in neighborhood theaters. It was as though Buffalo Bill's Wild West Show was coming to life right in front of these boys, each and every Saturday!

By the early 1920s, movies were the top form of entertainment in the land. Many motivated young men and women were eager to set sail for Hollywood and see if they had what it took to be a star in the blossoming industry. And young Markowski, athletic, handsome and full of boundless energy, was near the head of the parade.

Young Vincent Markowski

The man who would become Tom Tyler was born on August 9, 1903, in Port Henry, New York, the second of five children in the family of Frank and Helen Markowski. The brothers were Frank, Vincent and Joe. The sisters were Katherine and Mulvina (Mollie).

Frank Markowski Sr. was born in Lithuania and spent his early years there. Situated on the Black Sea and bordered by Latvia (north), Poland (west and south) and Russia (west), Lithuania came under Russian rule in 1795. The new rulers tried to change the country and brutal persecution and economic necessity forced thousands of Lithuanians to emigrate in the late 1800s. Some time near the end of the century, Frank Markowski was among those making the voyage to America, seeking a new life. He settled in upstate New York.

Port Henry was a section of the city of Moriah, which boasted a rich and versatile heritage. A hundred and twenty years earlier, many local soldiers had been given land by King George of England for their service in the French and Indian War. Iron ore was discovered, lumber and gristmills sprang up and farms were started. Huge furnaces were built in large factories, and the shipping of ore became big business, first by water and then by railroad.

Many families came to work in the iron ore mining industry, which flourished from around the early 1800s all the way until the 1970s. Mines were privately owned, then became the property of Witherbee-Sherman & Co., and finally in 1938, Republic Steel Corporation. Most of the large hotels, homes, churches, and schools were built in the early 1900s and many still exist today.

Port Henry was a fishing industry center in the years Vincent Markowski lived there and it is still a popular sport today. Once the lake freezes in January, little villages sprout up on the rivers around Port Henry as residents warm themselves with little stoves and holes are cut in the floors of shanties. Fishermen sit on benches and fish through the holes, whiling away the hours and, eventually, the years.

The town was also home to the infant movie-making industry. It boasted of a studio known as Arctic City and the famous serial, "The Perils of Pauline," was shot there in 1914. It starred Pauline White, an athletic woman who became a popular star of the era with her daredevil acting feats. Many of the stars stayed at the Lee House, a hotel on Main Street, which is still standing.

It is reasonable to assume that young Vincent and his pals were aware of the movie production and actually saw the serial in the town theater when it was released. He would have been just ten or eleven years old but it could have made a lasting impression on him; it may even have laid the foundation, conscious or otherwise, for his desire to eventually become an actor.

Both Frank Markowski Sr. and Frank Jr., Vincent's older brother, were employed at the Witherbee-Sherman and Republic Steel Corporation, toiling in the mines. It was tough and demanding work, and dangerous, as well. Frank Jr. was just sixteen when he began work there on June 25, 1917. But his time at the company was to be short-lived.

Always on the outlook for better working conditions for himself and a better lifestyle for his family, Frank Sr. heard about job openings at the automobile plant of Henry Ford in Detroit. He and his son left the mill on September 11, 1918, and shortly after the Markowski family moved to the Detroit area. They settled in a tight-knit Polish community named Hamtramck.

"Grandpa worked in the coal mines in New York, and Ford needed workers," said Ray Slepski, the son of Katherine, Tom Tyler's sister. "He came out here to Michigan for a better life. It was a grand opportunity."

Vincent was just fifteen at the time of the move and maturing rapidly. As a young teenager, he would have undoubtedly read or heard of the exploits of such famous athletes as boxers Jim Jeffries and Jack Johnson, wrestler Frank Gotch, football and Olympic hero Jim Thorpe and baseball stars like Shoeless Joe Jackson and, of course, the fiery Ty Cobb.

By the time the Markowski family arrived in Detroit, Cobb was on his way to establishing himself as the greatest hitter in the game. He had won nine straight American League batting championships from 1907 through 1915, and hit .382 in 1918. The next three seasons – from 1919 through 1921, when Vincent was living just a few miles from the Tigers' ballpark – Cobb was still knocking the hide off the ball, with averages of .384, .334 and .389.

When it came to personality, Vincent certainly was not at all like the hot-tempered Cobb. The Georgia Peach was well-known for badgering other players and for getting into tussles on and off the field. Vincent's mild manner was more in line with another great baseball star of the era, the superb Christy Matthewson, one of the greatest pitchers the game has ever seen. Matthewson was characterized by his quiet, unassuming personality and his modesty; that was how Vincent would be described for decades ahead.

Of sturdy Lithuanian stock, Vincent began testing himself in various scholastic sports and dabbling in weightlifting. But it's easy to imagine that he and his friends spent many a Saturday afternoon in the dark movie houses in their neighborhood watching the exploits of Fairbanks, Hart, Mix, Chaplin and others on the silver screen. In fact, athletic training and acting would eventually work together to mold a fabulous future for young Markowski.

According to reports, Vincent, like Ronald Reagan a decade later, was fascinated by acting and began envisioning himself up on the screen. He bought a theatrical make-up kit to experiment with changing his appearance. Even though he was shy almost to the point of being introverted, he wasn't afraid to dream big. Nor was he afraid, when he felt the time was ripe, to turn those dreams into action.

At some date in the early 1920s, when Vincent was nearly twenty years of age, he made up his mind that he was going to try and become a movie actor. The decision came as the result of an athletic contest that was held on the stage of the Martha Washington Theater in Hamtramck, one of three theaters in the city at the time.

One of the three theaters, the Star, was owned and operated by Leonard Slepski, who had married Katherine Markowski, Tom's sister. The Martha Washington Theater was owned by a friendly competitor, Florian Manteuffel.

"For some time, Manteuffel would hold stage shows during the weekends and I was told by my grandmother that Tom entered a weightlifting contest of some sort and won," said Tom Kozyra. "There was a talent scout sitting in the audience. He came up to Tom afterwards and told him he should go try Hollywood, and that he would give him some names of people to see once he got there."

Young Vincent apparently projected star quality even at a young age. And the movie talent scout wasn't the only one who noticed.

"My mother said she could remember that when she was walking down the street in Hamtramck with Tom, long before he left for Hollywood, girls would turn and stare at him as he walked by," said Ray. "Mom said he was so good looking even back then that everyone was taking notice."

Stirred by the talent scout's encouragement, Vincent decided to try Hollywood, even though it was a long, long way from Detroit. But his decision does not appear to have received much encouragement from his parents. According to family stories, it was his younger sister, Mollie, who spotted him the money to help him get started.

"Mom was younger than Tom and didn't have much money either," said Tony Redge, a son of Molly (Markowski) Redge. "But she was a very hard worker and saved every dime. She told me that she believed in Tom and wanted to help him realize his dream, and gave him a little money to help out. You know, people did things like that back then, for family members. Everyone tried to help everyone else."

Enlisting the support of a friend, Emil Karkoski, from the neighborhood, the two young men accepted the advice of Horace Greeley to "Go West, young man." They left Hamtramck in the summer of 1923 with little more than enough money to get them to California. They made it all the way to Denver, Colorado, together – but no further as a team.

"My father and Vincent lived in the same town (Witherbee) during their early years," said Tom Karkoski in December of 2003. "Both the Markowski (family) and my father's family moved to Detroit sometime between 1915 and 1920. That is a guess, as my father didn't talk much of his childhood or else I have forgotten what he may have related to the family.

"The one family story is that when Vincent decided to go to Hollywood to become a movie star he asked my father to go along. They worked their way across country, stopping in Denver on the way. The family story is that my father either lost his nerve or his wallet and returned to Detroit. He then returned back east to the Mineville/Witherbee area of northern New York, met my mother and got married and raised a family of eleven."

Strangely, the two friends seem to have never corresponded with each other again during the remainder of their lives. If they did, the members of Emil's family are not aware of it. The last real connection remaining is the oral tradition handed down for eighty years and one photo.

"The only other information I have is from my oldest sister, who said she wrote to Tom Tyler sometime in the 1940s but did not get a reply," said Karkoski. "I do have a picture of my father and Tom, probably taken sometime just before they left for Hollywood."
(4)

The details of Vincent's trip have long since evaporated but he may have stopped several times to take odd jobs to help pay his expenses. There were just 387,000 miles of paved road in the country back then and it took 13 days to reach California from New

York. At least one source of information has him working for a period in the mines near Pittsburgh, spending time at sea, and working as a lumberjack.

Indications are that the trip took several weeks, so one must assume he paused along the way, for short periods of time. But it seems improbable that he ever spent time in Pittsburgh or at sea. More than likely, those stories are products of the imaginative publicists hard at work behind small desks at some film studio, determined to make the leading men of the day appear to have led exciting, rugged lives before settling in the capital of make-believe.

More than anything, his refusal to turn back like his friend shows the determination and discipline that marked Vincent then, and would be a strong component of his personality all the remainder of his life. Vincent Markowski was not a quitter and he believed in himself and had the courage to follow his dream.

The Roaring Twenties

The third decade of the Twentieth Century, the era from 1920 to 1929, was an exciting time to be an American. The start of the 1920s ushered in an entirely new era for the United States. Fresh from victory in "The War to End All Wars," the growing nation was proud of its newly-earned status as a world power. Americans were anxious to reach out and grab a piece of the new and exciting lifestyle. The enthusiasm stretched from coast to coast, and to all spots in between. No place, it seemed, was immune from the upbeat mood reflected in a stunning array of new forms of entertainment.

It was called "The Roaring Twenties," and with good reason; there was bootleg booze, flapper girls, exciting new music and a new economic surge. Fads like marathon dancing and flagpole sitting were huge and Harry Houdini was thrilling audiences with his amazing escape artist routines. The major dances were the Charleston, the One Step and the Black Bottom!

Sports was entering its Golden Era with names like Jack Dempsey, Babe Ruth, Red Grange, Bobby Jones, Man O' War and Johnny Weissmuller constantly in the news. In 1923, Ruth was just coming into his own as baseball's premier star and Dempsey was the highly-respected heavyweight boxing champion of the world.

The nation was startled on August 2, 1923, when Warren G. Harding, the 29th President of the United States, died of a heart attack while visiting San Francisco. Woodrow Wilson took over as President. By then, prohibition was in its fourth year of a doomed experiment, and Al Capone was about to take over as the crime kingpin of Chicago.

And a new wave of excitement was taking wings in the cozy valley near Los Angeles that had become the focal point for moviemaking!

"The Twenties was an age of revolution in communication," wrote David Robinson in the book, *Hollywood: 1920-1970*. "American life was transformed in varying degrees and varying ways by the effects of cars, radio, advertising and the cinema. Americans in the Twenties were fascinated (and the fascination is nowhere more clearly reflected than in the movies of the time) with the New Morality." *(5)*

Movies played a tremendous role in shaping the nation's image of itself and in providing inspiration to millions of men and women to do something exciting with their lives. The screen was filled with dashing heroes like Douglas Fairbanks and Rudolph Valentino, and petite heroines like Mary Pickford and Clara Bow. Exciting, new fictional characters like Tarzan and Zorro made their debuts on screen, and comedians Charlie Chaplin and Harold Lloyd had patrons rolling in their seats with laughter. A long parade of cowboy stars stirred the imaginations of young boys everywhere.

That was the atmosphere that Vincent Markowski found himself in at the age of twenty-one.... raw, lean, muscular, handsome and very eager to gain a foothold in the movie industry. It was just three years after the start of the Roaring Twenties.

In the summer of 1923, Vincent finally arrived in California. Like thousands of young men and women before and after who aspired to crack the film industry, he discovered that there was a long stream of setbacks, disappointments and menial jobs ahead of anyone trying to establish a foothold.

In short, life was tough for those who arrived in Hollywood, hoping to make it big in the exciting world of movies. They were inspired by the wonderful stories they had seen back home on their movie screens. The boys figured they could ride, rope and brawl just like the heroes they were watching, and the girls hoped they could be as cute and appealing as the gals they saw up on the huge screen. Movies like "A Star Is Born" probably helped to inspire such dreams. But reality provided a rude awakening for such dreamers.

"Entertainment was what Hollywood offered in the widest possible variety, as thousands and thousands of pretty girls poured into town, particularly anxious to find work in motion pictures," wrote Roger Kahn. "Pathetically few ever did, even as extras. The dreamy nonsense of 'A Star is Born' is entertaining, but not finally believable. In it, a pretty hometown girl, helped by a brash but soft-hearted producer, finds stardom over a counterpoint of personal sorrow. Most of the pretty girls who did migrate to Hollywood found not stardom but rejection." *(6)*

Of course, the same could be said for the men who made it to Hollywood. The odds were astronomically against anyone making it as a movie actor, let alone becoming a star like Douglas Fairbanks or Tom Mix.

The cowboy movie phenomenon was well under way when Vincent settled into the young city by the ocean. The little film industry that had begun as a modest little venture in the teen years was riding high, thanks to a variety of men who were able to capture the hearts of the American public.

"America's favorite source of action on the screen was the Western. The West represented urban America's dream of lost innocence, of a pastoral freedom now sacrificed to hustle and the motor car.

However, "…by the early Twenties the Western had passed into its classic period, when the perennial formulas of the genre were laid down. Like almost any great tradition in popular drama, the Western has only one plot. Its appeal lies in the reassuringly recognizable form and force and morality of the story; its art consists in the skill with which variations are developed upon basic themes." *(7)*

That basic theme is that the good cowboy stands up for what is right and battles the evil forces around him, saving the day and the girl. It means, in essence, "the eventual defeat of the bad man through the moral and physical superiority of the hero." *(8)*

There were plenty of men anxious to fill that role for the dozens of film studios cropping up all along the California coastline. Western films were full of action, but had no sound. The film industry was still silent and the heavy emphasis on action in the western film was ideal for the new medium. Americans could hardly get enough.

"Unburdened by the limitations of still-to-arrive sound and the need to speak and act, a whole rash of Western heroes broke out in the 1920s. Actors like Harry Carey, Buck Jones, Hoot Gibson and Ken Maynard didn't have to do more than ride, punch and shoot," wrote one author.

"The Twenties saw, as well as much else, the development of the standardized, assembly-line film and the creation of the myth of 'giving the public what it wants.' What is astonishing is that so much of real worth came out of this cinema and this era."

The first sports star to try Hollywood was Gentleman Jim Corbett, who took the heavyweight boxing title from John L. Sullivan in 1889. He made several movies in the 1910 period and was a stage star for over a decade. Even Frank Gotch, the popular and handsome world heavyweight wrestling champion, took a trip to Hollywood in 1916 to see about appearing in some films. However, he was struck down by a mysterious illness and died in December of 1917, before movie arrangements were finalized.

Jack Dempsey was the first athlete of the Roaring Twenties to make the move to Hollywood in order to try motion pictures. As the dynamic, hard-hitting heavyweight champion of the world, Dempsey was the best-known athlete in America and Pathe Studios figured he would pack the fans in at the box office. In late 1919, he signed a contract with Pathe for a serial called *Daredevil Jack.* He received a ten thousand-dollar bonus, and a salary of one thousand dollars a week. He also endured a face job, as the studio bosses felt his battered features needed some sprucing up.

Dempsey's success paved the way for other athletic types to try the film world. And few could match the physical appeal of Vincent Markowski. Shortly after arriving in Hollywood, the young man from New York, by way of Detroit, was about to begin one of the most fascinating and intriguing film odysseys of all time. He would never become one of the golden boys of the film world or make a tremendous amount of money – but before he was done he would appear in over 150 movies, star in most of them, play two of the best-known super heroes in American history and stamp himself as an actor of astonishing versatility.

Goodbye Vince, Hello Tom

Driven by necessity, Markowski quickly found a small and cheap apartment off the beaten path to stay in while he began looking for work in Los Angeles. It was a far cry from glamorous but it served the purpose for a young man who was willing to cut corners and sacrifice for success. He worked any type of job he could to pay his rent and keep food on the table. He worked as a laborer and as a model, sometimes posing in the buff for sculptors and painters. He had already begun serious training with weights and in acrobatics and had developed a very muscular torso. He spent his spare time watching the trade papers for calls for any type of work at the numerous studios, big or small.

Shortly after arriving in Hollywood, Tyler befriended Oliver Drake, an aspiring journalist who would some day become both a screenwriter and a director. In his memoirs, Drake wrote about meeting Tyler back in those early days, when both were trying to make it. Drake recalled that Tom lived in cheap quarters and would walk from studio to studio in his indefatigable effort to land a job. He said that when Tyler was hard-pressed for money, Drake would often treat him to meals.

When Tyler finally made his mark with FBO, he did not forget the kindness that Drake had shown him. He played a key role in Drake receiving work at FBO as a writer.

Tom's very first film work came in a bit part in the 1924 movie called "Three Weeks," based on a novel by Elinor Glynn. It was produced by Metro-Goldwyn-Mayer, a large new film group formed when Louis B. Mayer joined forces with Metro-Goldwyn to become MGM. Somewhere along the line, he apparently decided that the name Vincent Markowski was not suitable for a film actor, because he appeared as Bill Burns during his early credits.

It's easy to imagine the excitement young Vincent must have felt upon walking onto his first movie set. Just a year and a few odd months earlier, he had been living in his parents' home on Mitchell Street in Hamtramck, dreaming of being a movie actor. Now, here he was… in Hollywood, actually employed by a studio. That small but important step was followed a few weeks later with another tiny part in another MGM film, entitled "The Only Thing."

Shortly after, word went out that MGM was planning to make a huge production of the very popular book by General Lew Wallace called *Ben Hur*. It was to be a biblical epic in the truest sense, and there would be many extra-type roles for young men with well-developed physiques who could play soldiers during the time of the Roman Empire.

Armed with photos of himself, Vincent arrived at the studio and snagged a spot in the production. Ironically, it was the very same story that had opened the door wide to the acting career of William S. Hart twenty-five years earlier. Hart had played the role of Messala, the main adversary to Ben Hur, in the New York stage production of 1899.

On the movie set of "Ben Hur," young Markowski caught the attention of an agent who was working for a studio called FBO (Film Booking Office of America), one of the leading producers of B westerns. FBO was a small, independent company that had been purchased by Joseph P. Kennedy when the previous owners went bankrupt. The studio was keen on adventure and action story lines that were very popular in an era when movie-goers were looking for thrills. Usually well done and full of action, the FBO westerns of the late 1920s provided the quality that the finest studios producing outdoor sagas would offer in the next two decades.

"Caught in some financial woes, the British R-C Pictures (Robertson-Cole) and their U.S. subsidiary, Film Booking Offices (FBO), were taken over in the mid 1920s by President John F. Kennedy's father, Joe Kennedy Senior," wrote Chuck Anderson on his terrific web site called *The Old Corral*. "Tom and scores of hopefuls lined up at the FBO portals for screen tests, and the good looking, muscular young man was singled out and put under contract for a group of western adventures with a starting salary of about $75 per week.

"Kennedy was a shrewd, profit-oriented businessman who realized the potential of the hastily made and inexpensive westerns. He already had Fred Thomson and his trusty cayuse, Silver King, under contract, but Thomson was demanding substantially higher production expenditures and a larger salary. Kennedy and little FBO couldn't (or wouldn't) knuckle in to the extravagant demands, whereby Thomson left to fail with his expensive westerns at Paramount.

"Little FBO, which was the forerunner of RKO Pictures, had Tyler as well as Bob Steele, Buzz Barton and Bob Custer. Tom Mix even did a few for FBO." *(9)*

Though the figures could vary widely, the cost for making a B western was usually stunningly low. Some were made for as little as $8,000 a film, and were shot in three or four very busy days, often of eighteen hours or more per day. The films were of about sixty minutes duration. A studio could gross up to $80,000 on a good film with a well-known star in the lead, and the demand was such that if they cranked out a dozen or more a year, a tidy profit could be realized.

Often, the determining factor for the final cost of the film was the fee the top star would demand. Cowboys and actors anxious to move into the industry and grab the top billing would work very cheap. The studio chiefs, known for their tight-fisted ways, were determined to keep costs as low as possible. The result was a constant haggling over salaries of the top stars.

Mix and his No. 1 rival, Buck Jones, commanded huge salaries, close to $17,000 a week at their peaks. But the studio bosses weren't happy about the tremendous salaries and soon were on the lookout for new cowboy types with whom to replace the high-drawing stars.

"The B westerns would develop a star system that existed completely outside of the rest of the Hollywood universe," wrote cowboy film expert Bobby Copeland. "Studio heads decided to raise their own stars in the Mix mold, tying them to contracts and paying them like slaves." *(10)*

"The B western was a child of poverty – a perfect vehicle for the producer working on a shoestring budget who could not afford a sound stage or construct lavish sets," wrote one film historian. "To make a B western, all he had to do was hire a few actors, rent a half dozen horses and travel a few miles outside Los Angeles, where nature provided the kind of spectacular scenery that could give an extra boost to even the most shaky productions."*(11)*

The western film formula was one that Mix had developed a decade or more earlier. Here is how Mix himself described it:

"I ride into a place owning my own horse, saddle and bridle. It isn't my quarrel, but I get into trouble doing the right thing for somebody else. When it's all ironed out, I never get any money reward. I may be made foreman of the ranch and I get the girl, but there is never a fervid love scene." *(12)*

In a casting call, Vincent would have certainly stood out from the crowd as much as Arnold Schwarzenegger did in the 1970s. Tall and lean, he had dark good looks and an engaging smile. He also had a sensational physique, as good as any male actor who had ever made his way to Tinsletown. Blessed with a genetic disposition toward muscularity, he had worked hard at weightlifting during his early twenties and the results were obvious for all to see.

Having lost its leading star, Fred Thompson, to a rival studio, FBO was searching for a handsome leading man who could play a cowboy hero. Markowski was invited to the FBO offices and impressed the men in charge. He was then asked point blank if he could ride a horse. The truth was that he had spent almost no time on a horse prior to arriving in Hollywood, but he wasn't about to lose such an opportunity with the wrong answer at this stage of the game.

"I said 'yes' and didn't even gulp," he said years later. "I knew if there was a way to stick on, I'd find it. I contacted a friend who was an expert horseman and it wasn't long before I was riding very well."

Once again, the intrepid spirit of Vincent Markowski came to the forefront. The young man who had come all the way to Los Angeles, completing the last half of the trip by himself, left the FBO offices in high spirits and spent the weekend at a nearby ranch learning to ride. By the time shooting started for "Galloping Gallagher," a new western hero was born. Vincent Markowski had become a horseman, and the studio changed his name to the phonetically pleasing Tom Tyler.

Just where the new name came from is lost in the mists of time, but the first name may well have been borrowed from Tom Mix, the most popular western star of the era. A story made the rounds years later that an FBO executive simply began thumbing through a phone book and when he saw the name Tyler, he liked it and presented it to Vincent, who agreed it sounded good enough.

The first major newspaper article about the new cowboy star was datelined out of New York. It got a few facts wrong, but still managed to excite the public about the prospects of Tom Tyler. It appeared on July 31, 1925.

Tom Tyler, a young man who was born as William Burns in Port Henry, N.Y. just twenty-two years ago, is the new "surprise star" who has been signed by Film Booking Offices to take the lead in a series of western pictures. He strongly resembles George O'Brien, built on a larger and more powerful scale.

Mr. Tyler is a team star of the Los Angeles Athletic Club, and has been appearing on the screen for less than a year. He has, however, already been spotted by film experts as a coming star and was offered an attractive con-

tract by Metro-Goldwyn-Mayer just the day after he had been gobbled up by F.B.O. He appeared in Elinor Glynn's "The Only Thing" and has supported Fred Thompson. He also played several roles with Joe Brown Productions and was featured in "The Midnight Express."

Tyler holds the American and world's record in weightlifting in two events. He is an expert horseman and spent much of his time on his father's ranch in Wyoming. He has also played a lot of football and is a track and field star of note.

F.B.O. seems to be specializing in world's champions. While the personnel of the big Hollywood studios does not include any fistic title holders, and there is no disposition on the part of the powers that be within the organization to annex any pugilists, almost every other department of athletics is represented by F.B.O. stars who are champions in their lines. Fred Thompson, Maurice "Lefty" Flynn, Dick Talmadge, Bob Custer and others all hold American or world's record marks, and now Tom Tyler has been added to the galaxy of "outdoor" stars. With his attractive personality, modest disposition, winning smile and a great screen presence and with the line of rattling stories which has been purchased for the new "surprise star" he should be a whale of a pleasant surprise for exhibitors and fans. "Let's Go, Gallagher!" is the title of the first Tyler production. It is a fast-moving western, replete with action and melodramatic thrills.

Another story that appeared in some California newspapers a month later, dated August 31, 1925, carried a headline that said, "Tom Tyler, Larry Kent and Alice Ardell new faces on F.B.O. lot." A photo of a very young Tom Tyler wearing a cowboy hat accompanied the story, which read as follows:

At the nucleus of what promises to be one of the largest film groups of new faces for the screen and new talent behind the megaphone, five stars and directors hitherto unknown in the capacities in which they are now engaged have been added to the personnel on the F.B.O. studios during the past few weeks.

General Manager B.P. Fineman believes in developing screen ability and directorial skills. It is his claim that the public has long wanted new personalities to entertain it, and that the best way in which to get something different is to break in new men... Tom Tyler, new stardom, is being directed by James Gruen, former Los Angeles newspaperman, and by Robert DeLacey, who was for many years a star cutter. They are now filming "Let's Go, Gallagher," a western picture.

The name of the movie was changed somewhat, and "Galloping Gallagher" was released on September 30, 1925, when Tom Tyler was just one month past his twenty-second birthday! The film did well at the box office, and Tom cranked out two more films before the end of the year – "The Wyoming Wildcat," released in November, and "The Cowboy Musketeer," released in December.

Though there is no existing correspondence to validate the point, one can imagine the surprise, and happiness, that greeted the news back home that the young man who had left Hamtramck for Hollywood had already starred in three films by the end of 1925. His circle of family and friends must have read or heard about Vincent with an excitement bordering on disbelief. And undoubtedly the neighborhood movie houses which he had frequented just two years prior were filled to capacity when the three FBO movies appeared there. Because of his courage to act upon his dreams, Vincent Markowski had completely turned his life upside down in a very positive fashion.

Two other members of the Markowski family decided to come to California and try their luck, as well. Frank Jr. moved out first and eventually started a long career in film as a gaffer and best boy. He worked in Hollywood for over three decades, mostly for Columbia Studios, and traveled the world in his job. He was in Hawaii for the making of the classic film, "From Here To Eternity." Frank Jr. even changed his name to Tyler.

"Everyone kept asking my dad why his name was Markowski if Tom Tyler was his brother," said Mike Tyler, Frank's son, in 2004. "So he finally said 'To hell with it' and changed his name to Tyler, too."

Sister Katherine also tried living in California. She shared an apartment with Tom, and found work with Pacific Bell. She stayed for nearly four years, eventually moving back to Hamtramck, marrying Leonard Slepski and raising a family. Ironically, Katherine and Leonard met at church in Los Angeles, when Leonard was in California visiting with his family. Tom and Katherine were always close and it was to her that Tom would turn for support when his health failed in the 1950s.

In 1926, the fastest rising young star of the western film industry was very active. Tom made eight more pictures for FBO, the last called "Flying U Ranch," which was adapted from a book written by the popular novelist, Bertha Mossey Bower. Not only was Tom staying busy, he was improving his acting skills with each effort and was pleasing his studio bosses. In addition, the handsome young man from Michigan was starting to gain a large national following.

"His riding got better with every film and his on-screen brawling came naturally," wrote Glenn Shirley in *Old West* magazine. "He not only held his own with other FBO cowboys – Fred Thompson, Bob Custer, Hoot Gibson, Bob Steele – but soon began surpassing them at the box office." *(13)*

The proof of his popularity could be found in the Exhibitors Herald publication of October 30, 1926. The article listed the "60 best box office names in pictures, according to a questionnaire signed and returned by 2,471 exhibitors participating in the survey conducted by "the studio section" of the Herald. Exhibitors were asked: 'What names mean the most to you in your billing?' The top 60 included Tom Tyler in spot No. 34! That was a remarkable rise to stardom for Vincent Markowski, just three years removed from Hamtramck.

Colleen Moore led the entire list with 278 points, while Tom Mix was second with 255, just three points ahead of Fred Thomson. Harold Lloyd was fourth with 249 points, followed by (in order) Hoot Gibson, Norma Talmadge, Mary Pickford and Douglas Fairbanks.

Tyler's 34th ranking placed him ahead of such established stars as Lillian Gish, Noah

Beery, John Barrymore, Rudolph Valentino, Clara Bow and western actors George O'Brien and Harry Carey.

By the start of 1927, Tyler was fully established in the film world. The 1927 exhibitors poll had him ranked ahead of such stars as Buster Keaton, Lionel Barrymore, Jack Dempsey, Tim McCoy, Bob Steele…and even Charlie Chaplin!

On July 23, 1927, a photo of Tom and FBO boss Joseph Kennedy appeared in the "Filmograph" magazine, with the following cutline: "Before going east one of the last things Joseph P. Kennedy did was to talk over the future of his new western star, Tom Tyler, with Tom and his director, Robert DeLacy. FBO has brought Tom to the front ranks among the western stars of the screen during the past year."

Ironically, Tyler remained in the film world much longer than did Kennedy. After a period of filmmaking and womanizing, including a torrid affair with legendary screen star Gloria Swanson, Kennedy left Hollywood in the 1930s and immersed himself in the world of politics. In 1934, President Franklin D. Roosevelt named him as the first Chairman of the Security and Exchange Commission. In 1938, he was appointed Ambassador to Britain, the first Irish-Catholic ever to hold the prestigious post. His political aspirations reached their zenith in 1961 when his second son, John F. Kennedy, was sworn in as the 35th President of the United States of America.

Tom Tyler (right) was still known as Vincent Markowski when he and his pal, Emil Karkoski (left) set out for California. Karkoski turned around in Denver and returned to Hamtramck.

(Photo courtesy of Tom Karkoski)

This is the home that the Markowski family settled into in Hamtramck, after moving from Port Henry, New York. Vincent was about 15 years old at the time of the move.

LEFT: Vincent Markowski was young, muscular and handsome by the time he arrived in Hollywood in 1923, seeking fame and fortune. He was destined to find the former, if not the latter.

RIGHT: Shortly after Vincent became Tom Tyler, he posed for this portrait, circa 1925.

One of Tom's earliest films was "Three Weeks," made by Goldwyn Studios in 1924. He was billed as Bill Burns in his extra role, but would become Tom Tyler for his next film, as the star of "Let's Go, Gallagher" for FBO.

Tom is seen in two very early studio poses here, probably in 1924 or 1925.

BELOW: "The Masquerade Bandit" was made in 1926 by FBO.

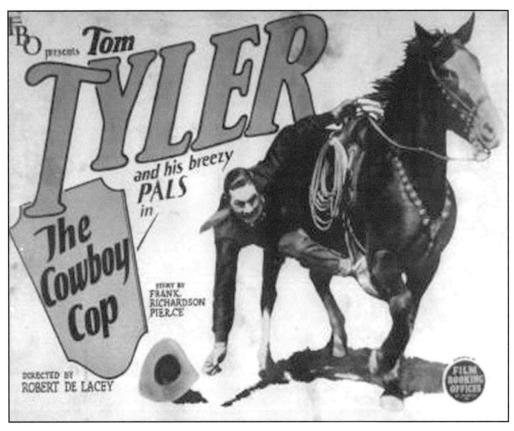

ABOVE: FBO wanted to make sure fans knew who the star was of its 1926 film, "The Cowboy Cop," splashing Tom's name in big print.

Tyler in a studio pose (left) and on an arcade card (right)

TOP: All through the 1920s, Tom made many films for a busy company called Film Booking Office (FBO). Here Tom (right) poses outside the FBO studio with the owner, Joseph P. Kennedy (center), who was the father of John F. Kennedy, the nation's 40th President, and director Robert DeLacy. Tom was paid $75 a week for most of his films at FBO.

In the 1927 film "Tom's Gang," by FBO, Tyler propped up a wounded Frank Rice. It was one of 29 films Tom made for the studio, all of them silent.

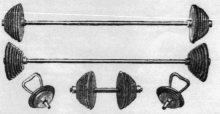
The January 1927 issue of *Strength* magazine, the nation's leading journal on physical fitness, carried a large advertisement featuring Tom Tyler. The ad said that Tom used Milo equipment to become national heavyweight weightlifting champion and set many records.

To bring in extra money, Tom posed as a model for exercise equipment in his spare time, and also flexed his muscles for the camera. These photos were most likely taken in the late 1920s.

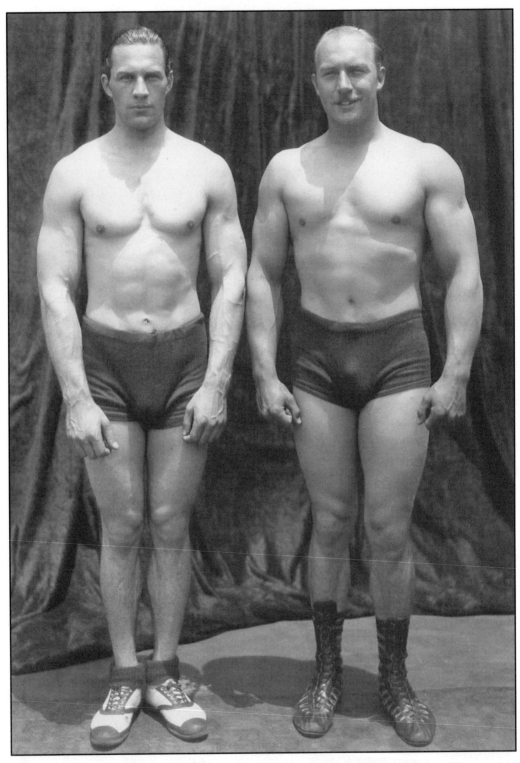

At his weightlifting peak, Tom Tyler (left) was considered the strongest man in America. Here he poses with a teammate from the Los Angeles Athletic Club after making the United States Olympic team in 1928.

Tom's imposing physique certainly was one of the best of his era. Although the "Mr. America" contest did not exist in the late 1920s, chances are very good that he would have won the title had the event been in existence when he was in his prime years.

Tom Tyler shows the form that made him the nation's top heavyweight weightlifter during the late 1920s.

ABOVE: Tom was teamed with the young Frankie Darro in a number of films for FBO, including "Gun Law."

BELOW: Darro (right) idolized Tyler and appeared in over 150 films during his long career.

Mixing Two Careers

Tyler's career was certainly influenced by Joseph P. Kennedy, and also by the leading cowboy star of the time. While Vincent Markowski may have borrowed Tom Mix's first name, it also seems possible that Tyler used Mix's example for staying in top shape as a motivating factor in his own film career.

"Tom's rightly-earned title 'King of the Cowboys' was never seriously threatened during the Twenties," wrote a biographer of Tom Mix. "This in itself is a tribute to Tom for he was then in his forties. He kept his body in excellent physical condition and he gave the rest of the boys a real run for their money. He exercised daily and seldom gained or lost more than a few pounds." *(14)*

Tyler was cut from the same mold as Mix. While building his career as a cowboy film star, Tyler was also building his strength and physique at a similar pace. He had joined the Los Angeles Athletic Club shortly after arriving in California, and was dedicated to regular workouts. His progress was stunning, and drew rave reviews from the most knowledgeable weightlifting expert of the era, David Willoughby.

An accomplished weightlifter himself, Willoughby became in later years the leading authority on the early days of the sport. In 1949, he wrote a long series of articles for a leading muscle magazine in which he discussed the sport during the 1920s. His admiration for Tyler is without restraint. Here is what he wrote:

> *During the year 1925, four more amateur lifters joined the L.A.A.C. team. They were Romaine Straight and Ernest Weber in the middleweight class; Max Allen, a light-heavyweight, and Tom Tyler, heavyweight.*
>
> *Tom Tyler, whose real name, I understand, was Markowski, was about as strong to start with as I was after having trained with weights for eight years. I gave him the benefit of my coaching and he rapidly improved in strength and lifting power. He had tremendous natural energy, but lacked in skill and balance. If he had persisted in developing to a high degree the latter qualities, he would have become one of the greatest lifters in the history of the sport.*

In the weightlifting competition of that era, the title went to the man who compiled the highest total in the three lifts – the military press, the snatch and the clean and jerk.

The military press is pure power. A lifter has to pull the barbell from the floor to the shoulders in one motion, and then ram it up overhead without using the hips and the thighs to boost it. The power has to come from the shoulders and arms.

The snatch takes considerable athletic skill. It is a very difficult move, requiring an athlete to squat over the bar and then ram it upward in one continuous motion. The lifter hurls the weight overhead and then stands up with it.

The clean and jerk consists of grabbing a barbell and pulling it to the chest, then ramming it overhead. Unlike with the military press, the lifter can use his legs and hips to thrust the weight upward and overhead, jerking the weight to arm's length.

Willoughby continued his praise for Tyler:

> *As it was, considering the period in which he lifted, and the fact that he trained in fits and starts rather than regularly and methodically, he did well enough, as the following review of some of his performances will show.*

> *In Tyler's first public appearance in competition, in the weightlifting championships of Southern California on May 28, 1925, he did a right hand clean and jerk of 199 and 3/4 pounds; two-hand snatch of 189 and 1/4 pounds; right hand military press of 85 pounds; two hands deadlift of 469 and 1/2 pounds (for) a total of 1,192 3/4 pounds.*

> *This performance was sufficient to win for Tyler the heavyweight championship with many pounds to spare.*

The competition took place just four months prior to the release of his first starring western role. His weightlifting success led to him being publicized in a photo in which he was wearing a bathing suit and black athletic boots, and holding a large piece of wood over his head. The caption underneath the photo read, "This is Tom Tyler, the strongest man in Hollywood who carries trunks of trees on his head and doesn't think anything of it. Tom is racing through 'Let's Go, Gallagher,' for F.B.O."

It was becoming obvious to one and all that Tyler was a man of considerable drive and energy, spending a great amount of time not only working toward a film career but building an athletic career, as well. A 1926 issue of the popular fitness magazine called "American Athlete" was equally enthusiastic in its praise of the new star:

"Tom Tyler is a perfect example of an all-around athlete. He scales 197 pounds in trained condition and is surprisingly fast of feet. Among his many accomplishments, he can perform an astonishing variety of acrobatic tricks and daring stunts on the horizontal bar."

Tyler won the AAU Southern California heavyweight championship four straight years – 1925, 1926, 1927 and 1928. In 1928, he also won the AAU national championship. But it was in 1927, the same year that Babe Ruth smacked a record sixty home runs, that Tyler set a record of his own. In August, weighing just 192 pounds, he clean and jerked 300 pounds, becoming the first American to ever go over the 300-pound mark in that particular lift. It was a landmark moment in weightlifting history, similar to breaking the four-minute barrier in the mile run.

Tyler's physique was as sensational as his lifting exploits. In a very impressive two-page advertisement for the Milo Barbell Company in the physical fitness magazine "Strength," Tyler is shown facing the camera with no shirt and arms folded across his chest. He looks to be in wonderful condition.

"Tom Tyler – first-class athlete, horseman, acrobat, movie star," blares the headline. The advertisement reads as follows:

Mr. Tyler is the national heavyweight lifting champion and he holds world's records also. His superb physique and unusual physical ability and versatility... have won him recognition among the motion picture companies of the West, which resulted in an actor's contract.

Look at those arms Mr. Tyler possesses. You would probably give anything within reason for a pair like them, and yet a pair of arms and body like Mr. Tyler's are so easy to obtain with a Milo bar....

Look at Mr. Tyler gracefully sitting his horse. Doesn't he look as though he always has plenty of energy to spare?

His measurements were very impressive for the day. He was listed at six foot two inches tall, at an even 200 pounds, with a 45-inch unexpanded chest and a 32-inch waist. He had thick, powerful arms and a well-tapered body, similar to what Steve Reeves, a former Mr. America and Mr. Universe, displayed in the 1950s when he rocketed into movie fame as Hercules. The first Mr. America contest was held in 1938; had it been held in the late 1920s or early '30s, chances are high that Tom Tyler would also have the title of Mr. America to add to his long list of credits.

He made eight movies in 1927 and six more in 1928. There was also a rumor of an impending marriage for the new star. The Los Angeles Times reported on May 9, 1928, that Tom was about to become engaged to actress Ethlyn Clair. However, she denied the report with the following quote: "It's a little too early to say anything definite. Tom and I are very dear friends but that is all I can say at the present. You had better see me some time later or ask Tom." The paper added that "Tyler couldn't be located for his version." Several months later, she wed another man and Tom continued his bachelor lifestyle. It would actually be another ten years before he married for the first and only time.

In late spring of 1928, he entered the Olympic weightlifting trials, hoping to earn a spot on the United States team that was journeying to Amsterdam, Netherlands, for the worldwide event. In the Olympic tryouts, held outdoors in the Coliseum at Los Angeles, Tyler made his best lifts. It was a spectacular performance for any day, let alone for 1928 prior to the advanced training and diets that have been employed since the 1980s. He set a new American record on his way to first place. His lifts included 230 pounds in the press, 230 pounds in the snatch and 300 pounds in the clean and jerk, for a total of 760 pounds. His total amount lifted stood as the American record until 1932.

Though he won the U.S. trials at heavyweight (with a minimum weight of 182 pounds), Tyler did not compete in the 1928 Olympics in Amsterdam. In fact, no American lifters went. According to a report in the book *The Iron Game*, the explanation is "that there were not any Americans good enough to compete in the Olympic Games." *(15)*

That's certainly an unfair assessment, based on Tyler's achievements. The top three lifters in the Amsterdam Olympics recorded totals as follows: The gold medal winner from Germany totaled 819.5 pounds, the silver medallist from Estonia lifted 792 pounds and the bronze medal winner from Czechoslovakia had 786.5.

According to those efforts, Tyler would not have won a medal in 1928 with his 760-pound effort. On the other hand, competing in such a top-level event usually helps an athlete improve his lifts, and Tyler would have needed just 27 pounds more on his total to win the bronze medal, which was definitely within the realm of possibility. Even a silver medal, requiring an overall increase of 34 pounds in the three lifts, might have been possible, but the gold medal was probably out of reach. It would have taken an increase of 60 pounds to accomplish that.

Ironically, three Americans who captured medals in Amsterdam in two other sports wound up in Hollywood shortly after the close of the 1928 Olympics. Johnny Weissmuller won two gold medals in swimming, Buster Crabbe earned a bronze in swimming and Herman Brix earned a silver medal in the shot put. Within a few years, all three were starring as Tarzan and all three enjoyed long and productive film careers.

Brix won six national shot put titles, one as a collegiate athlete at the University of Washington in 1927 and five AAU national titles. In 1935, Brix starred in two Tarzan films and many Tarzan "experts" consider him the best Tarzan ever. Afraid he would be typecast in Tarzan-like films, Brix changed his name to Bruce Bennett and began a very successful second career, basically as a leading man in B movies and a character actor in bigger films, taking much the same path as Tyler had.

Brix met Tyler in the mid 1930s and seventy years later still remembered the impression that Tyler made on him.

"Early on in my career, I made two movies with Tom's wife, Jeanne Martel, and I met Tom Tyler a couple of times," said Bennett in 1999. "While we were shooting 'Flying Fists' (in 1937, for Victory) Tom came over to the set and I talked a bit with him between scenes. He seemed like a very nice fellow, but rather quiet and reserved.

"Tom had a tremendous physique," added Bennett. "He was very powerful, probably the most powerful man in Hollywood at the time. In my opinion, he would have made an ideal Tarzan." *(16)*

A year after the Olympics, Tyler was still improving in his lifts. Willoughby lists the following efforts for Tyler in 1929:

- a one-hand swing lift of 177 pounds;
- a two-hand deadlift of 500 pounds;
- a right-hand snatch of 182 pounds;
- a right hand clean and jerk of 216 pounds (with a sense of balance he could have done 250 pounds, says Willoughby);
- a two-hands snatch of 231 pounds;
- a two-hands press of 230 pounds;
- a two-hands clean and jerk of 340 pounds.

The clean and jerk lift was truly amazing, as Tyler weighed around 200 pounds at the time – which means he could lift overhead 140 pounds more than his own bodyweight. It's hard to imagine any actor since then trying to grab a 340-pound barbell and pull it to his shoulders, then ramming it overhead with a jerk of the thighs and hips. Probably the only film stars who have ever been able to lift that much weight other than Tom Tyler were Arnold Schwarzenegger and Lou Ferrigno, two hard-core bodybuilders who weighed forty to sixty pounds more than Tyler.

It is beyond dispute that Tyler, while playing a cowboy hero on film in the late 1920s, was truly one of the strongest men in the entire world, a little-known fact by even those who have admired the man for decades.

The reason that Tyler "trained in fits and starts rather than regularly and methodically" was due to the other driving force in his life – his film career. Weightlifting was good, clean fun and helped mold his very impressive physique, to be sure; but it was the film work that would allow him to earn a decent living and to stay in California. Obviously, the film work had to take first priority.

Decades later, there were stories that Tyler had not only been a prominent weightlifter, but a wrestler, boxer and football player, as well. They were most likely embellished stories to help sell him to the American public as an exciting and athletic newcomer. One Tyler promotional sheet put out by Reliable Studios in the late 1920s said, "winning prizes in rodeos brought Tom to the attention of movie scouts and he headed for Hollywood only after extracting from them a promise that he would appear only in stories of the true West."

Of course, Tyler never learned to ride a horse before arriving in Hollywood in 1923, let alone win any rodeo prizes. It was just one of many examples of the Hollywood publicity machine run amok.

"I suppose it's possible that Tyler did all of that wrestling stuff, but my guess is that a lot of it was straight from the imagination of a studio P.R. man. Remember, he was competing with cowboys like Tom Mix, and Mix was a master embellisher," said Calvin Castine, a native of Port Henry who has studied Tyler's career for years.

"As time goes on, it becomes harder and harder to separate what was real from what was manufactured for the public. In his hometown of Moriah, the town supervisor told me his mother said that Tom rode out of town on a horse and the next time he was heard from he was in the movies. It's a nice story for the locals, but it's a long way away from the way it really happened." *(17)*

Ray Slepski, Tom's nephew and godson, was also skeptical of any such activities.

"As far as I know he did not do anything except the weightlifting," said Slepski. "If he did engage in any of these other sports, I am not aware of it. Of course, some of this could have happened prior to my birth or when I was young and perhaps never passed on or forgotten about."

The best evidence that Tyler may have been a wrestler of any regard comes from Joe Bonomo, a well-known strongman, stuntman and actor throughout the 1920s and '30s. Bonomo had a long background in both wrestling and weight training and in his autobiography mentioned briefly that Tyler was a wrestler and a strongman. Bonomo was very proud of his own tussling prowess, in boxing and wrestling, and it seems unlikely that Bonomo would have given credit to Tyler if he did not have some knowledge of his wrestling exploits.

In the popular serial, "Phantom of the West," made in 1931 by Mascot Studios, Bonomo is listed fourth in the credits behind Tyler, who has star billing.

"Tom Tyler, also a wrestler and a strongman, and I had a real opportunity for some outstanding rough-and-tumble fights in the Mascot serial," wrote Bonomo. *(18)*

Whether or not Tyler was a wrestler, boxer or football player will most likely never be known for certain. What we do know is that he was a terrific weightlifter, the best in the nation for several years at least, and might have been a wrestler of enough repute that a legitimate athlete like Bonomo would have known about it. Strength is, after all, an important ingredient for wrestling success, but not as important as is skill and/or technique.

The impressive Tyler physique translated very well onto the movie screen. No cowboy film star looked the part of a rugged hero more than Tom Tyler. He had also won the admiration of young fans through the use of Frankie Darro in his films of this era. The two were a public relation director's dream come true – a handsome, muscular leading man with a pleasing personality playing opposite an engaging boy who idolized him, on and off the screen.

"Out of oblivion and into the national prominence in three months is an unheard of procedure," blared a full-page ad in the Moving Picture World publication of Nov. 28, 1925. "But no one can deny that Tom Tyler, with little Frankie Darro and Napoleon, the mutt, have justified this tremendous advance ballyhoo accorded them."

"Darro's inclusion in supporting casts particularly pleased Tyler fans," wrote Shirley. "The lad's presence not only gave Tom a sidekick but provide motivation and a guaranteed 'out' for any predicament in which the hero found himself. By the same token, when young Frankie was not saving Tom from a dastardly villain's plot, it was because the boy had been kidnapped or otherwise endangered, giving Tom a chance to gallop to the rescue.

"Darro, who idolized Tyler, gave excellent performances and became a popular star himself in the 1930s." *(19)*

He also had an interesting life and career. Darro was born Frank Johnson in Chicago, Illinois, on December 22, 1917. His parents were aerialists for the Sells Brothers Circus and the family moved to California where Frankie made his screen debut, at age six, in the Wallace Beery feature, "Judgment of the Storm."

Due to his small size and youthful appearance, Darro played teenagers well into his twenties. Always a physical performer, he often did his own stunts, many times out of necessity as his small stature made it difficult to find stunt doubles his size. He also doubled other performers, including Leo Gorcey, and women. He was an accomplished horseman and made several films where he played jockeys.

From 1925 through 1929, he worked in twenty-eight films with Tyler and it was in those that he gained his early popularity. After Tyler, Darro worked with several other popular cowboy stars, including Harry Carey, Gene Autry and Bill Elliott.

During World War II, Darro served in the U. S. Navy. After the war, he returned to Hollywood and appeared in many films. As Darro got older, however, he found it increasingly difficult to secure employment, and by the late '40s was doing unbilled stunt work and bit parts. He opened a bar in 1951 and died at age 59, on December 28, 1976. He appeared in over 150 films, his last role coming in 1975.

In the late 1920s there was a huge challenge looming on the horizon for Tom and the other western stars of the era. The silent age of film was about to come to an abrupt end, and a whole new world was dawning.

"As the third decade of the Twentieth Century began, the great Western heroes of the silent screen found themselves facing a villain more deadly than any they had opposed on the screen to date: sound," wrote Alan Barbour.

"But there were several stars – six to be exact – who did adapt well to the new sound medium and who became the giant stars of the early Thirties: Buck Jones, Tim McCoy, Hoot Gibson, Tom Tyler, Ken Maynard and Bob Steele." *(20)*

That may have indeed been the case, but the transition wasn't exactly smooth, at least in the case of Tom Tyler.

The Sound Era

"The Pride of Pawnee," released in June of 1929, was Tyler's last film for FBO. Determined to include sound in its films, the firm was reorganized and became known as RKO. Its bosses decided to not renew Tyler's contract. At the end of the year, he was among several name actors given a sound test by Cecil B. DeMille for a key role in his film, "Dynamite." Tyler didn't get the role, but he was in good company: also testing and missing out were Buck Jones, Randolph Scott and Gordon Elliott.

After leaving FBO, Tyler signed with Syndicate Pictures to kick off the new decade. Syndicate was still making silent films, and his first eight films for the company were without sound. The inclusion of sound would, of course, alter the direction of the film industry for all time. No change was as big, and yet the studio system emerged at the same time and had almost as large an impact as sound.

As Tyler was setting weightlifting records, movie theaters were sprouting up all over America, with just about any town of any size boasting at least one small movie house. Often, a mid-sized town would have six or seven theaters, and the smaller towns began carrying twin bills, meaning two movies each day. They tried to change the movies at least twice a week, so there was a constant and large demand for B westerns.

In the 1930s, the nation had 120 million people and thousands of small movie houses. It was estimated that as many as 90 million movie tickets were being sold each week! Not even the devastating stock market crash of the 1929 era could stop the train of success that the movie industry was riding.

"If it had not been for the movies, the '30s would have been an even sorrier time for the average American," wrote Albert R. Leventhal in his book, *Those Fabulous Movie Years: The 30s* . "For from 10 to 50 cents you could see a double feature, plus a cartoon, plus a newsreel, plus (at the top price) an hour-long stage show headed by top talent – up to five or more hours in which to forget the endless waiting in long lines for jobs that didn't exist, the ominous letters from the electric company, the gas company, the phone company, the landlord, all saying the same thing: pay up, or else!" *(21)*

"….the public, gratefully and innocently, was hooked; and it was probably in part due to the revived enthusiasm for the cinema brought about by sound (as well as the cinema's proven value as an opiate for depressed societies) that carried the cinema industry safely through the stock market crash and the years that followed." *(22)*

By the start of the 1930s, Tyler was an established star. He had been in Hollywood since 1923 with forty-plus film credits, most of them westerns. Though most of them were quickie films, produced in a week or less, he was the star in over twenty of them. He wasn't making big money, but he had gained a certain degree of popularity, both with the kid fans across the nation and with producers who were anxious to produce quick and cheap films, usually for a total budget of $8,000 or less.

The folks who had known Vincent Markowski back in Witherbee, New York, and

Hamtramck, Michigan, must have been impressed with how far he had come in a very short amount of time. In fact, Tyler took time out from his busy schedule in 1931 to return to Hamtramck and turn up as the guest of honor at a New Year's Eve party for young boys. The local newspaper printed a photo of a smiling Tyler attired in a suit and holding a straw hat in his hands, with a story about the event.

Forty boys had as their guest of honor at a New Year's Eve party at St. Ann's Community House a man they had seen and heard often but who couldn't see and hear them until the party.

The man is Tom Tyler, Hamtramck boyhood's greatest movie hero. He is the hero of Hamtramck's boys because he is himself a Hamtramckan. Until nearly ten years ago, he played on the same streets that these same 40 boys romp around on now. He left home one day in search of greater opportunities and found them – nearly three thousand miles away in Hollywood. His prowess and horsemanship won for him a place in the hearts of millions of kids throughout the country, but no group of youngsters accorded his pictures a greater reception than those in his own hometown.

And New Year's Eve they showed their respect for him. His appearance at the party was held as a surprise for the boys, ranging from eight to fifteen years in age. When he entered the dining room, they immediately recognized him and sent up a tremendous cheer for him.

Tom Tyler had dinner with them and then addressed the assemblage. In his talk, he referred to them as pals and, in Popeye fashion, advised them to drink their milk. They complied with a toast of milk to him.

The 40 youngsters were entertained by the Opti-Line Club, a St. Ann's organization. It was the club's annual bit for charity and they topped it by inviting Tyler to the affair.

Back in Hollywood, some major changes were in store. While Syndicate was preparing to switch to sound, Tom hired out to Mascot Pictures in 1931 to make "Phantom of the West." It was a milestone in his career, as it was not only his first all-talking film but it was his first serial.

"The ten-episode play featured him alongside veteran performers Tom Santschi, Joe Bonomo and comic Tom Dugan," wrote Shirley. "Besides good characterizations, the picture had strong adult appeal, which was more to Tom's liking, and his pleasant voice assured him of success in the era of sound." *(23)*

Screenwriter Oliver Drake remembers that Tom had plenty of trouble in making the switch, and he worked diligently to remove his foreign accent.

"When sound came in, things were tough for me in the picture business, but my friend Tom Tyler was having it much tougher," wrote Drake. "He had a slight Lithuanian accent and it seemed no one wanted him for a talkie. He had to move out of his house in Beverly Hills, sold his car, and was slowly going down the drain. I finally convinced him to get with my friend, J. Frank Glendon, and see if Frank could help him lose his accent. I got them together and they began to work. Frank liked Tom very much and continued coaching him over the next few months, long after Tom's money ran out." *(24)*

Over the decades, all sorts of people – co-workers, business associates, friends and family members – remarked about Tom's pleasing personality and unassuming nature. His sincerity and humility attracted people to him time and again and made them eager to assist in any way that they could. Both Drake and Glendon were eager to help him, and that support probably saved his film career.

While working on his voice problem, Tyler returned to Syndicate for four more films in 1931 before landing the title role in a Universal serial with a grand story and solid cast. Tom was the lead as the famous scout in, "Battling Buffalo Bill." Also staring with him were Rex Bell, another B western star (who would eventually become Lt. Governor of Nevada), legendary stuntman Yakima Canutt, and character actors Edmund Cobb and William Desmond. For the role, Tyler grew a mustache, sported long, flowing hair and wore buckskins.

In one scene, he was given the opportunity to meet the greatest athlete in American history. Jim Thorpe won the Olympic gold medal in 1912 in both the decathlon and pentathlon events, and played six years of major league baseball. He was an All-American running back in college, at the Carlisle Indian School, and also was the first big star of professional football. But by 1931, he was earning his living as a part-time actor in films and putting on football kicking exhibitions around the country. A Native American, Thorpe played an Indian chief in the movie.

"It was a wonderful part," Tom said of his Buffalo Bill role. "I love the out-of-doors and the feel of a good horse under me will always give me a thrill, but this doesn't make me unfit for any but cowboy portrayals."

To prove that point, he accepted the leads in two more serials from Universal, stepping completely away from the cowboy image he had developed and nurtured over the past fifteen years. Interesting enough, even though he is thought of primarily as a Western star, only two of his seven starring serials were westerns: "Phantom of the West," a Mascot production in 1931, and "Battling with Buffalo Bill," a Universal release that same year.

His popularity was such that in 1932 and 1933 Universal starred him in three more serials. In the first, "Jungle Mystery," he played Kirk Montgomery, an intrepid game hunter in Africa. "How would you like twelve successive weeks of typical 'Tarzan' business?" asked one promotional piece for the serial. "The twelve episodes of 'Jungle Mystery' will do the trick!"

In the second, "Clancy of the Mounties," he was a Canadian Mountie on assignment to bring in the bad guys, and in the third, "Phantom of the Air," he played a pilot named Bob Raymond who is used to test a new device that could revolutionize aviation. The "phantom" was a remote-controlled airplane that Raymond was using to thwart a villain trying to steal the device.

All three were action films and fairly well received by the youthful film-going public. However, all three are lost to the public and no films survive. More than anything else, they bear testimony to the fact that Tyler was willing to take on any type of role and was capable of playing any type of hero. Those were qualities that would keep him regularly employed in the land of make-believe for another two decades.

Tom Tyler,
cowboy star

Life in the Thirties

"If a young man is going to get ahead, if he is going to reach the top, he must be all wrapped up in what he is doing," said Sam Goldwyn, a movie mogul of the first rank in the 1930s. "He has to give his job not only his talent, but every bit of his enthusiasm and devotion." It's advice that Tyler eventually took to heart. *(25)*

Having set numerous records and won a national title, he began to drift away from the weightlifting scene and devote all his time and energy to his film career. The entire decade of the 1930s saw Tyler working for a variety of studios, crisscrossing back and forth. He started out the decade with Syndicate, then switched to Mascot, then moved back to Syndicate, then to Universal. He cranked out some good films for Mascot, then worked for Reliable Studios. Finally, it was back to his old FBO studio, now known as RKO. Obviously, the goal was just to keep working, often for meager salaries.

With Reliable Studios, he was given star treatment and his name was featured on the large billboard on the outside of the large building located at the corner of Sunset Boulevard and Beachwood Street. Two other stars, Jack Perrin and Richard Talmadge, shared billing on the large sign with Tyler, but his name was listed first. The studio was run by Bernard B. Ray and Harry Webb. During the two years Tyler worked for them, he made 18 films, most of them shot for around $8,000 per film.

But he was not progressing steadily in the areas of credit with the major film directors and producers of the time so that he could secure a breakthrough role, like Gary Cooper had found in "The Plainsman." Cooper had his first film role in 1925, just a year and a few months after Tyler's debut, and had landed strong roles in "The Virginian" in 1929 and "Farewell To Arms" in 1932. But his biggest breakthrough came while playing Wild Bill Hickok in the Cecil B. DeMille epic, "The Plainsman," in 1937. It's the kind of role that Tyler could also have handled, based on his strong (albeit brief) performances in other classics such as "Stagecoach."

Though Tom was the main star at Reliable Studios, that status wasn't doing much to advance his career. Author Don Miller, in his book *Hollywood Corral,* does not speak highly of the Reliable films of the era. While discussing the career of Bob Steele, who teamed with Tyler in the 1940s for the Three Mesquiteers series, Wilson charges that Reliable actually hurt Tyler's career.

"Metropolitan Pictures (Steele's new boss) was the company of Harry S. Webb and Bernard B. Ray, who took turns producing and directing and by this time were excelling at neither function. Their former company had been known as Reliable, which belied its name, and they had been responsible for Tom Tyler's drop in prestige." *(26)*

The fact was, Tom was making enough money to stay ahead of the game but was not seeing the kind of roles that could help advance his career into the higher echelons of stardom. His contract in the '30s was in the neighborhood of $400 to $500 a week, a good living to be sure but a far cry from the money Mix was making a decade earlier, and that major stars were drawing at the time. Much of the problem may have been his agent. Hollywood agents play a huge role in the success of their actors, and one wonders how adept he was at finding the big roles for Tyler and landing them for him.

At least one film critic stated his opinion that Tyler was capable of much greater successes had he been given the opportunity to show what he could do: "The feeling persists that with creative and intensive guidance, the attributes of Tom Tyler, buried as they were under an avalanche of neglect and carelessness, could have been transformed into a screen image approaching the highest plateaus," wrote Don Miller. "That it didn't happen is too bad."

"The '30s saw the star system reach its peak," wrote Leventhal. "At a time when factory workers and white-collar employees were drawing salaries that ranged from $40 to less than half that amount a week, scores of starred players drew from $3,000 to $10,000 or more per week." *(27)*

And the movie star lifestyle was changing, said Leventhal: "Unlike the big stars of the '20s, they no longer spent their money building huge mausoleums like Pickfair (the legendary home of Mary Pickford and Doug Fairbanks) on the fringes of Sunset Boulevard. Now the movement was away from Hollywood and bit farther out – to Beverly Hills and Pacific Palisades or Coldwater Canyon. One or two-story ranch houses equipped, of course, with pool and tennis courts, were coming into vogue, but the acreage was reduced, the lawns and gardens less lavish." *(28)*

Tom had purchased an attractive Spanish style home in Hollywood and sent several photos back to family members in Hamtramck. He posed in front of the adobe walls and small gate, wearing a big smile. At least on one occasion, several Markowskis visited him in his new home. Many photos were taken, showing family members and Tom enjoying the reunion.

For a period of time, he tried selling real estate in an effort to bring in more money. In 1934, he became partners in a firm called "Willett & Tyler Realtors" which was located at 771 North Vine. Tom was proud enough of the venture that he sent a photo back home to his sister, Katherine Slepski. The photo showed him standing in the doorway of the business, under a large sign with the name of the firm on it. But the business didn't amount to much and his main source of income continued to be his film work.

Physically and as an actor, the mid-1930s were his prime years. In the 1934 film, "Silver Bullet," made by Reliable Studios, Tyler looks to be the epitome of the western star. Tall, lean, ruggedly handsome and thirty-two years old, Tyler is at the peak of his game physically – and it's difficult to imagine an actor more suited to play the grand hero of the Old West.

In "Silver Bullet," Tyler rides into a rough town on a black horse and dressed entirely in black, including his hat. He is bumped into immediately by a rowdy and a brief fight takes place, with the rowdy flattened quickly. Moments later, Tyler walks into a general store and sees the same rowdy and two others picking on the young, pretty clerk (played by Jayne Regan). Tyler intervenes, drawing his pistol and shooting the hat off one man to make his point. The gal is very impressed, of course, and introduces Tom to her blind father. In short order, he is named sheriff of the town.

The action follows quickly and through it all Tom Tyler plays the role of western film star to perfection. He moves confidently through every scene and looks terrific on screen. Equally quick with his fists and with a smile, Tyler has all the potential to become one of the top western heroes of the era, maybe of all time. "Silver Bullet" is a terrific B western and showcase for the star Tom Tyler might have become. Some of his stunt work in the 1930s was being handled by Kermit Maynard, who was of a similar build and was the brother of Ken Maynard, a top star in the western genre.

Late in 1934, Tom was able to work in a visit to Hamtramck, just his second trip back home since leaving in 1923. Once again, his arrival was big news in the local press. The December 28, 1934, edition of the Hamtramck Citizen carried a front page photo of Tom with his mother and father, and a long story headlined, "Tom Tyler, screen star, visits parents."

> *While staying here, Tom will make a personal appearance in Hamtramck at the midnight show on December 28 and 29 at the Martha Washington Theater. The program will feature one of his best western pictures, 'Silver Bullet,' with 'Lightning,' the wonder horse. It is an honor to have a former resident of Hamtramck of Polish (sic) descent that has become a famous stage and screen personality to make a personal appearance in his own hometown.*

> *On December 25, the Hamtramck Citizen was honored with an exclusive interview at the home of his parents. Tom was found surrounded by his most ardent admirers, the parents and other family members.*
> *"If I had known I was going to stay two weeks I would have brought my wonder horse, 'Lightning,' with me (said Tom). I am very glad to have this opportunity of staying with my parents over the holidays.*

> *"As to Hollywood, it is a beautiful place with many beautiful buildings, wonderful landscapes and climate. The movie industry, since the drive for decent pictures on the screen, has produced more western and pioneer pictures as they are morally decent and appeal to the older people, as well as the children. The western pictures are going to be the main factors in the coming years. I am on my way to New York now on business to make arrangements for pictures.*

> *"I am making a personal appearance at the Martha Washington Theater, which will give me a chance to meet with all my friends and admirers. I also wish to send my sincere wishes for a Happy New Year to the Hamtramck exhibitors and fans."*

There is a hint of an intriguing development in Tyler's private life at about the same time. Just prior to making "Silver Bullet," he made a film called "Rio Rattler," also for Reliable. His female lead was Marion Shilling, who debuted in films at age nineteen. She found her niche in westerns and worked with ten "B" cowboy stars, including Tyler. Interviewed for the book *Western Women*, published in 1999, she offered a tantalizing tidbit:

Tom was, she said, " a handsome, big mass of muscle. Always prompt and knew his lines but very quiet. He was in the midst of a torrid love affair with Marlene Dietrich and during the day was probably in 'recovery.'" *(29)*

Dietrich, born in Germany in 1901, was one of the most erotic actresses of all time. Her 1930 film, "The Blue Angel," made her a worldwide celebrity and she came to Hollywood that same year to star in a series of films for Paramount. She and Tyler may have been on the same par as far as physical attractiveness, but they were on different planets when it came to salaries. By 1937, Dietrich was the highest paid star in the world, drawing as much as $500,000 per film. But she was, according to one biographer, also "one of the most bored...."

"She entranced moviegoers for more than three decades, and was every bit as enigmatic offscreen as the leggy femmes fatales she essayed on-screen," wrote movie critic Leonard Maltin. "Her numerous affairs with both men and women were ill-kept secrets, yet she managed to avoid scandal with more success than most, and was content to have her private persona shaped by her public one."

In 1935, when Shilling said Dietrich and Tyler were having a torrid affair, she was making "The Devil is a Woman," and "Desire," both considered highly erotic films for the era. There are no other sources that offer such an insight, but Shilling's recollections have a certain ring of truth to them. After all, Dietrich was well known for numerous affairs of a wide assortment, and it seems certainly possible that such a high-powered sex symbol might have found the outstanding physique and subdued personality of Tom Tyler worth pursuing.

Tyler had two other interesting roles in 1935, at opposite ends of the spectrum. In RKO's "Powdersmoke Range," he played a villain; the film was actually the very first in what was to become the Three Mesquiteers series, and starred Hoot Gibson, Harry Carey and Bob Steele. One western film historian says the film is considered a milestone in the genre but was rather lacking in anything noteworthy... other than Tyler's work.

"Nor are the performances anything to brag about, except Tyler's," wrote Don Miller, author of the excellent book, *Hollywood Corral*. "As a cold-eyed gunman who is persuaded to come over to the side of the law. Tyler was legitimately good and showed here what, in proper hands, he was capable of doing." *(30)*

Also in 1935, Sam Katzman was looking for western stars for his newly-formed Victory Pictures Corporation and came after Tyler. Katzman has earned a reputation as the master of the quick and cheap film, and was well known for not paying his people very well. Still, Tom accepted the lead role in "Rip Roarin' Buckaroo," which offered a very unusual storyline.

The movie begins in a boxing ring, where the hero Scotty McWade (Tyler) appears disoriented. He gets knocked out and is carried to the dressing room, where it is revealed he was drugged while in the ring.

McWade comes to just in time to see his opponent and two other men disposing of the drugs and he attacks them, knocking all three out with one punch each. Disgusted by the shenanigans, McWade leaves the boxing world to seek work on a ranch. There, he meets a girl (played by Beth Marion, a beautiful young actress), sings a few lines (of "Home On the Range"), punches out the ranch foreman, wins a horse race, and winds up in a boxing ring, where he scores a knockout victory to save the day.

Tyler is shirtless several times during the film and displays a very impressive physique, with rippling stomach muscles and powerful shoulders and lat muscles. But it is obvious from the boxing scenes that he is not a natural boxer; he is stiff and awkward in the sequences. As Willoughby had noted concerning Tyler's weightlifting efforts, Tyler "had tremendous natural energy, but lacked in skill and balance." The same could be said for his boxing in "Rip Roaring' Buckaroo." Based on what is seen there, it is doubtful that he had boxed much any time prior to that.

Some western film historians have noted the same lack of natural abilities in many of Tyler's fight scenes:

"Oddly enough, Tyler was not adept with the punches, and it was usually a disappointment to see Tom fanning the villain to slumber, when it was expected that he would break him like a matchstick," said Don Miller. *(31)*

By 1936, Tyler had been acting for a dozen years and had made a very positive impression on the nation's western film fans. His good looks and extremely impressive physical manner were top notch, and he certainly had as much charisma on screen as Hoot Gibson, Ken Maynard and Buck Jones. He even approached Tom Mix in sheer screen presence.

Yet he never made it into the "top ten" list of western stars as a solo performer. When looking at the list and seeing such names as Dick Foran, Buster Crabbe, James Ellison and Russell Hayden, the exclusion of Tyler is hard to understand. He did make the list three times, however, as a member of the Three Mesquiteers group, along with Bob Steele and Rufe Davis.

The best explanation is that Tyler was perhaps a bit past his cowboy peak when the poll was initiated in 1936 by the Motion Picture Herald. He had his first starring vehicle in 1925 and by 1936 had starred in approximately fifty western films. Had the poll come out in the late 1920s or early 1930s, he would have certainly made the top ten.

The first poll listed the following stars: 1. Buck Jones, 2. George O'Brien, 3. Gene Autry, 4. William Boyd, 5. Ken Maynard, 6. Dick Foran, 7. John Wayne, 8. Tim McCoy, 9. Hoot Gibson and 10. Buster Crabbe. Even Tom Mix was not listed, though he was still making films and was probably the best-known western film star of all time. By the way, Autry became No. 1 the next year and remained there for six straight years, until entering the service during World War II.

"In reality, the poll only measured the popularity of B-western stars as rated by the theater operators," explained western film authority Bobby Copeland. "While most B-western historians will probably agree that the top two or three stars in each year's poll do reflect the top money-makers, many will also agree that the rest of the rankings were purely guesswork." *(32)*

Other top cowboy actors who never made the list were Monte Hale, Lash LaRue, Jimmy Wakely and Whip Wilson.

There is another reason Tyler might have not made the list in the viewpoint of the theater operators, according to western author Bruce Hickey.

"Tom Tyler was stuck with bottom-dollar productions in his solo starring westerns, and never had a standout series," wrote Hickey. "Tyler's reputation is enhanced because he was a Mesquiteer, but more so for his classic portrayals in his serial career." *(33)*

Even though he did not make the top ten of western stars, he was very popular with his co-stars. Years later, several of them spoke candidly about what it was like to work on the set of a movie with Tom Tyler.

Karlton LaHue, who authored the book, *Winners of the West*, held Tom in great esteem. He was, said LaHue, "a likeable hero with a low-key personality on screen. Tom held his own with FBO cowboy stars and shortly began to surpass them at the box office. His riding became better with each film. The Tyler style of action was relaxation, so much so that many were convinced he could not act." *(34)*

Levine, who hired Tyler for "Phantom of the West," spoke highly of his star in an interview late in his life: "I do know he was a nice human being, a gentleman, never gave us any trouble and was always cooperative." *(35)*

Tom also was appreciated by most of the women who appeared in his films of the 1920s and '30s. Jean Carmen was his female lead in "Born to Battle" in 1935 and the rugged star made quite an impression on the attractive blonde.

"I made one picture with Tom Tyler," said Carmen many decades later. "He was a pleasant fellow – handsome, very tall and strong. He complimented me on my riding ability. Really, I had been riding for quite some time and was a better rider than Tom.

"I had a crush on him but he was involved with someone else at the time. I enjoyed very much working with Tom. I would have liked to have made more pictures with him." *(36)*

The "someone else" may well have been Marlene Dietrich, as Tyler had not yet met the young actress he was destined to marry.

Beth Marion, who starred with Tom in "Rip Roarin' Buckaroo," also enjoyed her time spent with him during the filming, and also offered an explanation for his voice which seemed high and a bit squeaky at times.

"He was a very handsome fellow," she said decades later. "He drove me back to town one time. We had a nice, long visit. I always thought, more than over-pronouncing his words, he maybe had a little accent and was trying to overcome that." *(37)*

Lois Collier appeared in seven Mesquiteer films with Tyler. She called him a "real quiet, nice man…" which was the general opinion of everyone who worked with him.

In 1936, Tom Tyler was at the top of his game, in many respects. His film career was doing nicely, if not spectacularly, and he was certainly drawing the attention of many starlets. He was in excellent health, a physical Adonis and making a good living in his chosen profession.

Some Big Changes

The following year saw tremendous changes for Tom. The cowboy singing craze that Gene Autry had fueled was well under way by 1937. So in "Lost Ranch" Tyler was called upon to sing a couple of tunes. However, it is obvious that his singing was dubbed. Some have speculated that the voiceover may have been the work of an actor named Glenn Strange, who became fairly well known in the 1950s for playing Sam the bartender in "Gunsmoke."

Early in the year, while making "Santa Fe Bound" for Victory, Tom met his female lead, Jeanne Martel, for the first time and she made a lasting impression on him. Slim and beautiful, she was compared by some to the very popular Joan Crawford. Within a few short months, they were married. Tom and Jeanne eventually made three films together, including "Lost Ranch" and "Orphan of the Pecos," both for Victory in 1937.

That summer, Tyler hit the road for several months as the star of the Wallace Brothers Circus. Cowboy heroes like Tom Mix, Hoot Gibson and Buck Jones had toured the country to promote their image and give fans a chance to see them up close and in person. It also provided them an opportunity to earn extra money between films, always an important consideration for any actor, regardless of stature.

The circus gave Tyler a chance to display his strongman abilities, as well as gymnastic stunts he had developed through his many years of strenuous workouts. An attractive poster, trimmed in bright red, showed Tom wearing his cowboy hat, pistol in hand: "Most famous of all Western Picture Stars," read the headline, with the name "Tom Tyler" in huge print.

A photo of the Wallace Brothers Circus company posing together, taken on July 24, 1937, in Aurora, Illinois, shows 96 workers. As the headliner, Tom is seated in the center of the third row, wearing a black cowboy hat and white shirt, and sporting a big grin. Beautiful women are on each side of him, with several clowns in front of him.

"When his quota for Victory was completed he joined the Wallace Brothers Circus," wrote Glenn Shirley. "His weightlifting, daring stunts on the horizontal bar and Wild West acts became the 1937 season's big draw under the big top." *(38)*

That same year, Tom learned that his sister, Katherine, had a baby boy and she invited him to be the godfather and come to the christening in Hamtramck. He accepted and also sent Katherine a telegram through Western Union, with big news of his own. The telegram arrived at St. Francis Hospital on the evening of September 8, 1937.

"Best wishes to you and boy. Hoping you are getting along in health. Am getting married tonight 7 p.m. – Love, Tom."

Tom Tyler and Jeanne Martel were married by a Lutheran minister at the Little Church of the Flowers in Forest Lawn Memorial Park on the evening of September 8, 1937. His agent, William Mickeljohn, was best man, and Jeanne's mother, Mrs. Edward Lauterback, was matron of honor. Oliver Drake, the screenwriter who had helped Tom when he first arrived in Hollywood in 1923, was an usher, along with Tom's brother, Frank Jr. Twenty people signed the guest book and a reception was held at the home of Dr. and Mrs. Stetson Humphrey in Los Angeles.

According to the article in the Los Angeles Times, which was accompanied by a large photo of the newlyweds walking down the aisle, Tom and Jeanne left the next day to join the circus in Atlanta, Georgia.

Sixty days after tying the knot, the couple made big news when they came to Hamtramck for a Markowski family reunion. One local newspaper printed a photo of Tom, dressed in a dark suit and sporting a wide grin, holding his newly-born godson in his arms, with Katherine Slepski at his side. "It's Another Fan for Tom Tyler" read the headline. The cutline added:

> No one can tell what will be the likes and dislikes of Raymond Leonard Slepski when he grows up but it's a pretty safe bet to say that his favorite actor will be Tom Tyler, star of western pictures in the silent days. Tom is a Hamtramck lad, having lived on Mitchell Avenue with his parents before his invasion of Hollywood – and the hearts of red-blooded kids. Before his return to the movie capitol to begin production of "Santa Fe Bound," he was the godfather of Raymond at christening ceremonies held at the Transfiguration Church on Sunday.

Another newspaper carried a long story on the celebrity newlyweds, under a headline that declared, "Beauteous Jeanne Martle Returns as Mrs. Tom Tyler." The following story was written by Leona Pilarski, who apparently had trouble with the last name of Tom's new wife, spelling it Martle rather than Martel.

> Tom Tyler came back to Detroit and Hamtramck Friday – back with his beautiful bride of two months. And she's just the kind of girl that Tom would marry – beautiful, violet-eyed, titian haired and so much like Joan Crawford that they could pass for twins!

> Her name is Jeanne Martle and the "Martle" is pronounced like "Martelle."

> Tom's family caught its first glimpse of her Friday and she lived up to every expectation. She is the slender, willowy type, with as lovely as figure as one could imagine. She wears her hair in a long bob, and represents the ultimate of the word 'chic.'

> Naturally, Tom's crazy about her. Because, after all, Tom is 32 years old and he has seen thousands of the screen's most beautiful and attractive girls. And thousands of girls have wanted Tom as husband.

> It doesn't make any difference how many times a person sees Tom Tyler in the pictures. He can't be appreciated until he's seen in person. He's as handsome as they come and has a pair of shoulders that an All-American football tackle would admire. And it would take a girl like Jeanne Martel to

"land him."

And according to Jeanne, he wasn't hard to land. In fact, both Jeanne and Tom say that theirs is a plain case of love at first sight. They saw each other at first on the set of the Victory Picture studios in Hollywood, where both were working on a picture.

They were introduced and had a date and just five months later they were married – married in a "church-around-corner" type of wedding. Their honeymoon was a short weekend and then they went back to work again.

The first thing that they had in the way of a honeymoon was this weekend. They came by train to Detroit to take part in the christening of Tom's nephew, Raymond Leonard, son of Mr. and Mrs. Leonard Slepski, 13358 Moenart Avenue. They came direct from Hollywood – arrived here Friday and left Monday. They even had to "cheat" to get this short respite from their film work. But their real honeymoon is just ahead of them.

"In a couple of months, when I finish my next picture, we're going to Honolulu for a real wedding trip," Tom said Sunday as his lovely wife smiled at him. "We would have waited to get married but both of us decided we simply could not."

Jeanne is much younger than Tom. It wasn't so long ago, when Jeanne was nine and ten years old, that she lived in Detroit. Tom didn't know her then. She left Detroit when ten years old and did not return until Friday with her handsome husband.

She lived in the East until she went west to Hollywood and started her climb, which may find her some day in the same ranking of the star she looks so much like – Joan Crawford.

"She's a grand little actress," Tom said. "She has everything any of the stars have and she'll keep right on going places. It won't be long before I'll have to hump to keep up with her. But I'm mainly interested in Jeanne as the grand wife she is and not the great star she might some day become."

Tom had many photos taken of him and Jeanne and sent them to the family. On the back of one shot, which showed his young wife fixing her hair and wearing a patterned swimsuit, he scrawled a brief note: "I call her Punky."

After nearly a year of touring with the Wallace Brothers Circus, he returned to the movie capital. The circus experience apparently took a toll on Tyler's work production as he made just one film, "King of Alcatraz," in 1938. In retrospect, that may have been the pivotal two years in his career. He made twelve movies in 1935, eight in 1936, six in 1937 but just one in 1938. After five films in 1939, he had been in Hollywood for sixteen years and had 102 films to his credit. If he was ever going to make the jump to the level of a major star, time was starting to wear thin.

In contrast, John Wayne had been making films for almost ten years by the end of 1938, with nearly 70 films to his credit, most of them B westerns, too. He started out life as Marion Morrison in Winterset, Iowa, on May 26, 1907. His family moved to California when he was seven years old, and he enrolled at the University of Southern California in the fall of 1924 and earned a position on the USC football team. Three years later, he was spotted working on the set of a Tom Mix movie and, like Tyler, was picked to star in B westerns.

Wayne bounced around in a number of minor roles in non-westerns, then made three serial westerns for Mascot Films and a series of cheap westerns for other small companies. At that point in his career, Wayne appeared stuck in a rut and many believed he would never really amount to much in the movie world.

"Duke felt he was condemned to be just a 'cheapie' actor in 'cheapie' Bs," wrote a biographer. "As 1937 was ending, John Wayne looked back on a dreary past and contemplated a dark future, He was now thirty years old, long past his prime when an actor should expect to be playing leading-man parts." *(39)*

Ironically, the turning point in Wayne's career came in 1939, and in a film that Tyler would have a key role in, as well. Of course, Tyler's role was much smaller and would not be the star vehicle that the film was for Wayne. While he was busy cranking out Tyler-type westerns, Wayne was also making friends with some powerful people in the business, including John Ford. He was often invited to spend weekends with the powerful director and his pals on Ford's yacht, drinking, fishing and playing cards. When Ford signed on to direct "Stagecoach," he picked Wayne for the key role of The Ringo Kid.

"Stagecoach" became a classic and led the way for Wayne to become a major star. Tyler played the villain, Luke Plummer, who was shot and killed by the Ringo Kid near the end of the movie. Tyler's acting has been mentioned for decades as a terrific piece of work in the brief scene.

"In the small but effective part of one of the deadly Plummer boys…. Tyler made his few minutes onscreen count for all they were worth, and more. He also developed the stylized 'long walk' after getting plugged, although (director John) Ford didn't show it – just Tyler ambling into the saloon after the gunfight, smiling benignly at the gathered tipplers, then keeling over." *(40)*

That same year, Tyler had an even smaller role in "Gone With the Wind." The movie adapted from Margaret Mitchell's run-away best-selling novel is considered by many to be the greatest film ever made. It certainly was the blockbuster of its generation and has survived the test of time. It was nominated for 13 Academy Awards and won eight, including Best Picture. It also was given two more honorary Oscars, for a total of ten. Estimates are that it has grossed nearly two hundred million dollars since its release in 1939.

Starring Clark Gable as Rhett Butler and Vivian Leigh as Scarlett O'Hara, it was three and a half hours in length and is a cultural phenomenon that has endured through the decades. According to film author Alan G. Fetrow, Tyler played a confederate officer during the evacuation of Atlanta. *(41)*

He is on screen little more than the blink of an eye but has one of just fifty speaking roles in the cast of two thousand, five hundred. About halfway through the film, when Atlanta is being evacuated, Scarlett runs into the street to see the confederate soldiers and civilians leaving the city. Amid the chaos, she spots Big Sam (played by Everett Brown), the black slave who worked at the Tara plantation where she grew up. She hurries up to Big Sam and talks with him briefly. Then an officer (Tyler) rides up and says, "Sorry, ma'am, we've got to march." Tyler is wearing a slight beard but one can still recognize the steely stare beneath the gray officer's hat.

He also appeared in "Drums Along the Mohawk" in 1939, a popular film starring Henry Fonda. A year later, he was appearing in another Fonda vehicle, "The Grapes of Wrath," which was the adaptation of the famous John Steinbeck novel about the great dust bowl of the 1930s.

His first film of the new decade, in 1940, was "Brother Orchid," a gangster movie starring Edward G. Robinson. He appeared in seven films during 1940, the fifth being "The Mummy's Hand." For his role as the mummy, he was wrapped from head to foot in a thick role of bandages. The effort paved the way for Lon Chaney to take it to the next level and become a film legend with the role.

Here is how one e-bay seller described the film:

" 'The Mummy's Hand' was the first of four sequels Universal made to their classic, 'The Mummy' (1932), that went on to become a staple of the Universal sequels and other later imitators – the slowly shuffling, bandage-enwrapped title figure, tana leaves, reincarnated princesses, mummification as punishment for forbidden love. Ancient Egyptian cults are wielded into quite an effectively fervid atmosphere.

"It is here, rather than 'The Mummy,' that they began. Interestingly, it was the sequels rather than the original that created the template for the genre cliches. And it is this story, 'The Mummy's Hand,' which the rest of the sequels take themselves from.

"Best of all is Cecil Kellaway (here billed as Cecil Kelloway)'s roly-poly stage magician, he having some charming moments pulling tricks while drunk. Peggy Moran's peppery determination also registers well. The mummy when risen (played by former stuntman and serial and B Western star Tom Tyler) also maintains a quite sinister effect, where Tyler has been shot in sinister close-up with blacked-out eyes. Indeed, the character of the mummy maintains much more threat in these scenes than the stumbling creature in all the other sequels put together. Combined, all of this gives the film a snappiness and appeal that the sequels lack."

Like the rest of the nation's film fans, Tyler was undoubtedly shocked by news that arrived in the morning newspapers of October 13, 1940. Tom Mix had been killed the day before in an auto accident south of Florence, Arizona. The flamboyant star was driving his Cord at high speeds when it flipped and he was pinned beneath it, dying instantly of a broken neck. He was sixty years old and his passing marked the end of an era for western films. But far bigger changes were on the horizon, not only for the movie industry but also for life in general, all around the globe.

Everything was turned upside down on December 7, 1941, when Japan bombed Pearl Harbor, catapulting American into World War II. After the U.S. entered the war, a new selective service act made men between 18 and 45 liable for military service and required all men between 18 and 65 to register. The terminal point of service was extended to six months after the war. From 1940 until 1947 – when the wartime selective service act expired after extensions by Congress – over 10,000,000 men were inducted.

Many of the nation's biggest film stars and sports figures went off to war – actors like Jimmy Stewart and Frankie Darro, and baseball stars like Bob Feller and Ted Williams. Tyler was just thirty-eight when the war broke out, yet he wasn't pressed into service, for one reason or another. But his career seemed to be going nowhere if not downward. He was suddenly reduced to playing second and third roles in the Westerns where other cowboys were the stars. In the 1941 Hopalong Cassidy film, "Border Vigilantes," he was a second-tier bad guy, taking orders from Victor Jory. Tyler is shot and killed about ten minutes from the end.

At this stage in his life, Tom had been in the acting profession for seventeen years and he wasn't focused on becoming a major star as much as he was on earning a solid living. He was in Hollywood to work, on a regular basis, not to be a prima donna waiting only for the most appealing roles. He proved it by working in a wide variety of formats.

"Tom Tyler was one of the few cowboy stars who was able to leave his horse behind from time to time in order to play non-western heroes," wrote Alan Barbour in his book, *Days of Thrills and Adventure. (42)*

Near the end of 1941, he appeared in the Abbott and Costello comedy "Buck Privates," made by Realart Pictures, Inc., along with another top-notch former athlete, Nat Pendleton. Like Tyler, Pendleton owned a national AAU title, but his came in wrestling. He was also a silver medal winner in wrestling in the 1920 Olympics in Antwerp, Belgium. Tyler's role in the film is very small. Halfway through the movie, the hapless Costello is duped into a boxing match. Tyler plays the ring announcer, a military man attired in white sweats. In a nice touch of irony, he introduces Pendleton as the referee – a former AAU national weightlifting champion introducing a former AAU national wrestling champion!

After a string of small parts, Tom may have felt his starring days were behind him. But his career was about to be resurrected in a stunning way. A new and dynamic type of hero was about to soar across the movie screens of America, and the muscular Tom Tyler was the perfect choice to play the red-clad powerhouse.

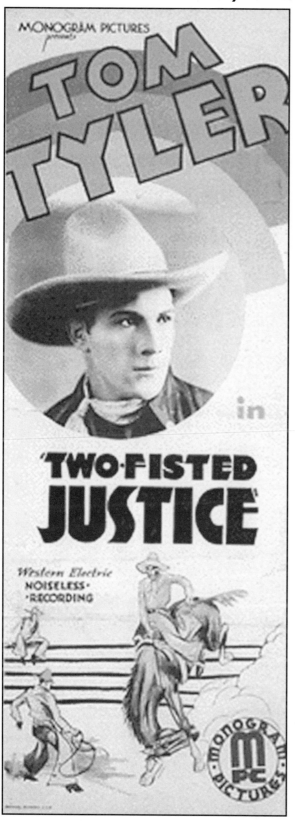

LEFT: "Two-Fisted Justice" was a 1931 film, one of eight that Tyler starred in for Monogram.

BELOW: Tom and a dog were featured in this small collector's card made in Europe.

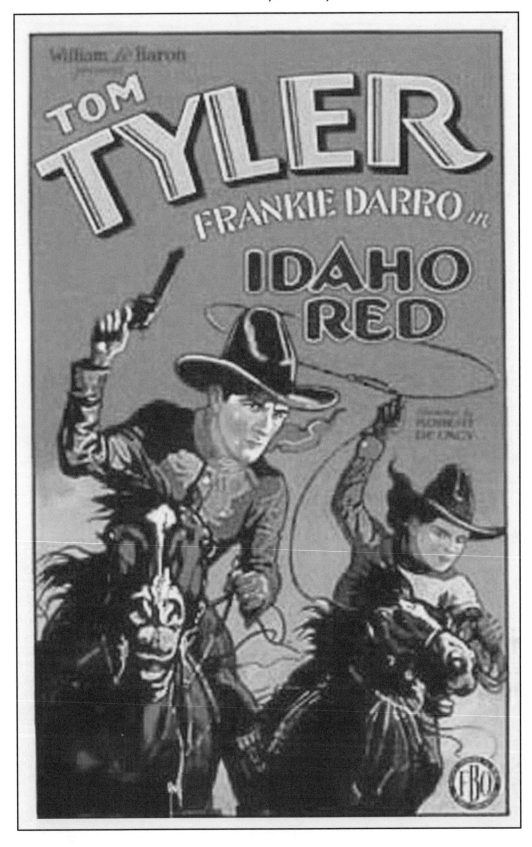

"Clancy of the Mounted" was a 1933 serial produced by Universal. Tom made an ideal mountie and was on the cover of a British magazine called "Boy's Cinema2."

RIGHT: Also in 1933, Tom starred as a pilot in the popular serial, "The Phantom of the Air." It was another Universal production.

While making "Battling with Buffalo Bill," in 1931, Tyler had the opportunity to work with Jim Thorpe (left), who played an Indian chief in the serial by Universal. Thorpe won the Olympic gold medal in 1912 in both the decathlon and pentathlon and was a star running back in football and a major league baseball player, as well. In 1950, he was voted by the AP the top athlete in American history.

There were always plenty of pretty girls around for the cowboys of the B westerns to rescue, and Tom's films were no exception. He posed with Alice Dahl (above) in "The Man From New Mexico" and with Lucille Brown (right) in the popular serial, "Battling With Buffalo Bill."

In the 1936 film, "Rip Roarin' Buckaroo," produced by Victory, Tom plays a boxer who loses a fight when he is drugged, and then turns his back on the sport and becomes a cow puncher. He winds up back in the ring and avenges his loss and saves a ranch, all at the same time. As shown in the photos above, the film gives Tyler the opportunity to show off his tremendous physique in a number of scenes, but the film aslo shows that his boxing skills are somewhat lacking.

Fighting the bad guys was
a prime ingredient of any
Tom Tyler film, whether in
the ring (above), or in a
crowded room (right) or
out on the range (below).

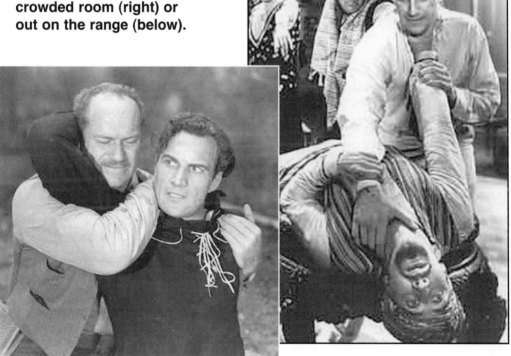

ABOVE: This lobby card from the 1935 movie "Unconquered Bandit" showed Tom at his best. The film was produced by Reliable, where Tom was the top star.

LEFT: While travleing with members of his family during a visit to California, in the 1930s, Tom posed for this candid shot.

(Photo courtesy of Mike Tyler)

ABOVE: Tyler made 18 films for Reliable Pictures Corp. in the 1930s and was featured on the main billboard at the studio's headquarters on the corner of Beachwood and Sunset Boulevard.
(Photos courteys of the Robert Webb family)

BELOW: Tom battles with a foe in the 1936 film, "Fast Bullets."

ABOVE: Tom poses outside his Beverly Hills home in the 1930s.

BELOW: Tom stands outside his realty office at 771 N. Vine in Hollywood. He dabbled in the buiness for about a year.
(Photos courtesy of Ray Slepski)

TOP: Tyler was the steely-eyed outlaw Sundown Saunders (left) in "Powdersmoke Range," a 1936 film made by RKO. The movie was the first in the popular Three Mesquiteers series and starred Harry Carey (shown here holding a dying Sundown Saunders), Hoot Gibson, Bob Steele and other stars of the B western.

In the 1937 movie, "Brothers of the West," Tom lands a right punch to the chin of villain Jim Corey. The film was made by Victory and Tom, dressed in all black, was at his peak as a cowboy star.

TOP: Tom worked with Jeanne Martel in the 1936 film, "Santa Fe Bound" and posed with her off camera (below). The next year, they were married.

Tom Tyler and Jeanne Martel were married at the Little Church of the Flowers in Forest Lawn Memorial Park on September 8, 1937.

(Photo courtesy of Mike Tyler)

TOP: Jeanne sits on Tom's lap during a visit to the Markowski home in Hamtramck shortly after the wedding.

LEFT: Jeanne and Tom relax during a swim outing in Tom's old hometown.

BELOW: Tom and Jeanne chat with a family friend in Hamtramck.

(Photos courtesy of Ray Slepski)

MOST FAMOUS OF ALL WESTERN PICTURE STARS!

TOM TYLER

APPEARING IN PERSON AT EVERY PERFORMANCE

WALLACE BROS. 3 RING CIRCUS

LEFT: Tyler hit the rodeo circuit shortly after being married and posters like this promoted his appearances.
(Photo courtesy of Fred D. Pfening, Jr., and Chuck Anderson)

BOTTOM: Tom and Jeanne spent their honeymoon traveling with the circus.
(Photo courtesy of Susan and Tony Redge)

While touring in Moline, Illinois, Tom temporarily swaps his horse for a policeman's motorcyle.

Tom salutes a fan at the end of one of his rodeo shows.
(Photo courtesy of Susan and Tony Redge)

It's Another Fan for Tom Tyler

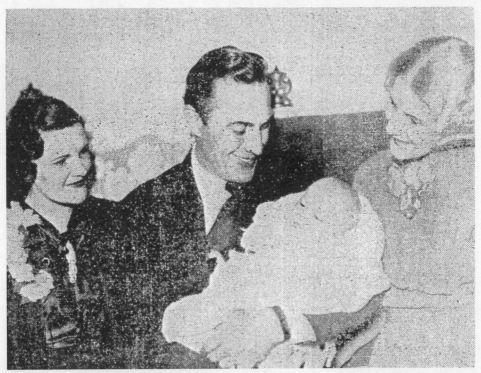

No one can tell just what will be the likes and dislikes of Raymond Leonard Slepski when he grows up, but it's a pretty safe bet to say that his favorite actor will be Tom Tyler, star of Western pictures in the silent days. Tom is a Hamtramick lad, having lived on Mitchell Ave., with his parents before his invasion of Hollywood—and the hearts of red-blooded kids. Before his return to the movie capitol where he is slated to begin production on "Santa Fe Bound", he was the godfather of Raymond at christening ceremonies held in the Transfiguration Church Sunday. Left to right are Angeline Kowalewski, the godmother; Tom and Raymond, and Mrs.. Leonard Skepski, mother of the child. The Skepski's reside at 13158 Moenart Avenue.

TOP: Tom holds his young nephew Ray Slepski while his sister, Katherine Slepski, and Ray's godmother, Angeline Kowaleski, watch. Tom was Ray's godfather. The picture appeared in the local newspaper when Tom and Jeanne visited Hamtramck in 1937.

LEFT: Tom and Jeanne relax at home.

(Photos courtesy of Ray Slepski)

In 1939, Tom had a very small role in one of the most popular films of all time, "Gone With The Wind." He played a Confederate officer who rode up to Scarlet O'Hara, played by Vivian Leigh, and told her it was time for her people to move on.

Flying High Again

In the mid-1930s, comic-book heroes made their first appearances on the silver screen. While most of the films prior to that era featured characters from novels, from history or from the imagination of screenwriters, the sudden rise of and popularity of comic books and dime action novels began to play a large role in the movie-making process in Hollywood.

"The tremendous growth in the popularity of the newspaper adventure comic strip in the mid-thirties was bound to inspire the serial producing film companies to bring America's new fictional heroes to the screen," wrote Alan Barbour in his book, *Days of Thrills and Adventure (43)*

The trend began in 1934 when Universal Pictures made a serial called "Tailspin Tommy," which was about the airplane daredevil. Following in quick succession were the Flash Gordon serials starring Buster Crabbe. Other newspaper heroes making the jump to the silver screen included Ace Drummond, Jungle Jim, Buck Rogers, Don Winslow of the Navy, The Adventures of Smiling Jack, and Dick Tracy. Tarzan actually debuted on the screen in 1918 but was getting top treatment in the 1930s, with a total of eight movies in that decade, with four different actors in the starring role!

Universal led the way by taking a total of sixteen comic characters into movies! But to Republic Studios goes the honor of making the best super hero serial of the era.

The "Adventures of Captain Marvel" is, in the opinion of many fans of the genre, the finest serial ever made. It was produced in 1941 by Republic Pictures in twelve chapters, with Bill Witney as director. It came about despite an intense rivalry between Captain Marvel, the super hero clad in red, and Superman, the super hero attired in blue.

Superman first appeared in comic-book form in June of 1938 and began on the radio February 12, 1940. An extremely powerful being from a far-distant planet, he had a dual identity and was able to leap (not fly, that came later) great distances in a single bound. With his bright blue uniform, bulging muscles and black-haired good looks, he was an immediate sensation. The popularity of Superman helped make comic books as a whole extremely successful in the following decades.

Captain Marvel made his debut in Whiz Comics in February of 1940 and was very similar to Superman, with several glaring exceptions. First, he was attired in a bright red uniform (as opposed to blue) with a bolt of yellow lightning on his chest. Secondly, he didn't receive his super powers from another planet in a far-off galaxy, but by a stunning metamorphosis which occurred when a young boy (Billy Batson) uttered the word "Shazam." A bolt of lightning struck him, turning him into the huge powerful super hero.

Shazam was the name of an ancient wizard who selected Billy Batson to receive the incredible honor of becoming Captain Marvel. The wizard's name was taken from a list of historical and mythological heroes and Captain Marvel was given the powers of each: the wisdom of Solomon, the strength of Hercules, the stamina of Atlas, the power of Zeus, the courage of Achilles and the speed of Mercury. Strung together, the first letter of their names spelled Shazam.

"The front office had been negotiating to buy the *Superman* comic strip," said Bill Witney decades later. "We were all looking forward to making it into a serial, and we sure it would be an all-time winner. We had started to look for an actor to play Superman and had interviewed every bodybuilder in or near Hollywood.

"It was late in the afternoon about four weeks before we were to start shooting when we were told we couldn't make a deal with the Superman people."

At that point, it may have appeared that the project was on death row, but that was far from the case. The bosses at Republic simply made a big shift, moving from one super hero to another in no time at all.

"After all the hassle with Superman being canceled, I couldn't believe the front office buying what I thought was an infringement on the Superman title," said Witney. "It was called Captain Marvel. I hoped the Superman people would hold off a lawsuit long enough for us to make the serial. A lawsuit did come along. They tried to stop Republic from releasing *The Adventures of Captain Marvel*.

"I remember a deposition they took from me. My theory was that both Superman and Captain Marvel infringed on the creator of *Popeye the Sailor Man*. Clark Kent in a phone booth, changed clothes and became Superman. Billy Batson said 'Shazam' and became Captain Marvel. Popeye came years before them to set precedent. He ate a can of spinach and his muscles bulged and he became Superman and Captain Marvel rolled into one.

"I don't know if my theory helped, but Republic came out on top of the lawsuits." *(44)*

After looking at a number of bodybuilders and husky actors, Witney and the producers selected Tyler for the lead role. It was a choice that has been applauded far and wide for six decades.

"Tom Tyler fit the part to a 'T,' " said Witney years later. "If I had to cast the part over again, I'd look for his clone."

Frank Coghlan, Jr. won the role of Billy Batson, boy reporter, and Nigel de Brulier played Shazam. Those were the only characters that made the crossover from the comic books. The other characters in the film were making their first appearance. De Brulier was superb as the white-bearded old wizard and his work was completed in just one day. Coghlan had more screen time than anyone else. The former child actor played the young man who was turned into Captain Marvel every time he said the magic word, "Shazam!" The transformation of Billy into Captain Marvel was pure magic in the comic books. It was a real tribute to the Republic team that they were able to make the screen transformation appear so credible. It was a sequence that came off well on the screen.

"I stood in front of a trough of flash powder that was ignited electrically by a prop man," explained Coghlan. "When the smoke enveloped me, the cameraman would cut. Then Tom Tyler would take my place, the camera would turn, and the smoke charge would be set off again.

"There were times on outside locations, when the wind was blowing from an unfavorable direction, that I lost a few eyebrow hairs from the unexpected powder flash in my face. After the film editors did their splicing, the transformation was very credible." *(45)*

The story takes place in a remote section of Siam and revolves around the efforts of a hooded villain, the Scorpion, to steal six optical lenses that when aligned together could turn ordinary stones into gems. Captain Marvel, working with the Malcolm Expedition, is called upon to thwart the Scorpion and his henchmen, and protect the expedition, too. There were twelve different chapters, all ending with a nerve-wracking situation for one of the heroes or heroine. The chapters were given exciting names, as well: 1 - Curse of the Scorpion, 2 - The Guillotine, 3 - Time Bomb, 4 - Death Takes the Wheel, 5 - The Scorpion Strikes, 6 - Lens of Death, 7 - Human Targets, 8 - Boomerang, 9 - Dead Man's Trip, 10 - Doom Ship, 11 - Valley of Death and 12 - Captain Marvel's Secret.

Filming for the twelve-part production lasted just thirty-nine days! It began on December 23, 1940 and finished on January 30, 1941.

"That kind of speed took top-notch teamwork, and Republic definitely had it," said Billy Benedict, who played Whitey, a young man, in the serial. "Directors William Witney and John English worked together as a team; both were remarkable men. Great men to work with and for. Believe me, we moved like the wind. We worked hard, but we still had a lot of fun." *(46)*

Benedict's background in films was incredible. He made his debut in 1935 and by the time he was finished, he had appeared in over one thousand films, two-reel comedies and television shows.

Republic Pictures gave the film the appearance of a more expensive production than its limited budget would afford. The use of stock footage from several other motion pictures, along with the special effects produced by the Lydecker brothers, Howard and Ted, made a big difference. And so did the incredible stunt work of David Sharpe, one of the best stunt men in Hollywood history.

"Dave was an absolutely fearless man who made even the most difficult stunt look easy," Coghlan said. "He was such a meticulous performer that he was rarely injured. I attribute this to his careful planning and his excellent timing and judgment of distance. My favorite caper that Dave did in Captain Marvel was in the first chapter when he did a back flip, catching two of the native tribesmen under their chins with well-placed kicks.

"And I'll never forget the day he made a headlong dive off the side of a cliff, dressed in the Marvel costume, into a small fireman's net far below, just to get the right camera angle impression of flying." *(47)*

"Bringing a superhuman hero to the screen in a manner that the audience would accept was a difficult business, and Republic brought all their powers to bear in filming *Adventures of Captain Marvel*," say the authors of the book *The Great Movie Serials*. "The result is unquestionably one of the finest movie serials ever made…" *(48)*

The authors were high in their praise of Tyler in the lead role.

"His angular face, piercing eyes and slender frame perfectly matched the very first appearance of Captain Marvel in the comics." They noted that the comic version of the Captain became much thicker and larger later on. They added, "while the stern-faced Tyler did not reflect the good-humored do-gooder Captain Marvel was in cartoon panels, he seemed perfect for the screen. He was holder of a world weightlifting title, making him *literally* one of the strongest men in the world. Although identified primarily with Westerns, he was not so much a cowboy but simply a *hero* type." *(49)*

It was an excellent point. Tom Tyler did indeed look the hero type, about as much as any actor in Hollywood history. He had the physique, the carriage, the mannerisms and, apparently, the true nature of a hero in all that he did. Tyler was in many of the scenes and the pressure was on to look good in the skin-tight uniform. He was employed for just four weeks of shooting – at the pay of $250 a week. Even though he looks magnificent in the role and the serial is lionized as among the three or four best ever made, he was paid a mere $1,000 for all his work. Today, that paltry figure seems incredible!

"Much of Marvel's success was due to the performers," declared one author. "Casting the late Tom Tyler as the mighty muscleman was sheer genius. Visually suitable, he did such a great job and is so well remembered by fans for this very role that it is difficult to imagine any other actor in his place." *(50)*

Despite all the adulation, Tyler wasn't perfect. He did have some drawbacks, according to at least one source: "The one criticism his co-workers always make about Tom Tyler was he was clumsy," said the same authors quoted above. "His lanky arms were always knocking over props, and in fight scenes, many times Tyler would accidentally connect with a punch that was, of course, supposed to narrowly miss. While he was magnificent for looking heroic in the close-ups (no one but the most hardened cynic would say Tom Tyler looked silly in that red outfit), much of the action, particularly the flying scenes that looked absolutely real, were performed by stuntman Davie Sharpe..." *(51)*

But Sharpe himself understood the importance of making the action scenes look real and fully understood that there was more to it than just his superb athletic skills. He knew that Tyler was a true professional who would work extremely hard and endure tremendous hardships in order to make the scene look legitimate.

"The one who should really be praised is Tom Tyler," said Sharpe many years later. "He spent hours strung up in that harness and rigging while being photographed in front of a process screen, and the pain must have been almost unbearable. Yet, he never let out a peep. What a pro!" *(52)*

Tyler faced a similar ordeal during the making of "The Mummy's Hand" when he was in the title role. It took nearly six hours for makeup man Jack Pierce to get Tom ready for work, wrapping him in yards and yards of bandage-type material and applying the thick makeup to his face.

"When the job is done, Tyler is so uncomfortable he can only work for three hours," wrote a reporter.

The advertising campaign for the Captain Marvel serial was terrific. The studio went all out to inform movie-goers that they were about to see something brand new on the screen. It was the first production to ever deal with a super hero who could fly and lift trees, and Republic spared no superlative in promoting the film. "See the amazing feats of Captain Marvel. He flies like a bird! Bullets bounce off his body! He is the most awe-inspiring character ever seen on a screen! A one-man blitzkrieg!

"Your eyes won't deceive you! You'll actually see Captain Marvel – ward off a machine gun barrage with his hands... hurl a 20-ton engine at his opponents... lift a giant tree with one hand... break through a wall of steel."

It was revolutionary stuff for 1941 and the crew, from top to bottom, was determined to pull it off. The public ate it up. The serial was a big success and over sixty years later was still being called the best serial of all time. There were many elements to its success, of course, but none was as important as the proper casting. Tyler was the perfect super hero, both physically and in his portrayal, and to him goes the lion's share of the credit for the success of the venture.

As good as the effort turned out to be for Captain Marvel, the film was still a serial, which was considered to be the lowest rung of the movie stepladder. In some instances, working conditions were little better than what a slave would expect, and the status was low. So was the pay. In fact, some B western stars even had it in their contracts that they could not be forced to work in serials!

"At a large studio you would have a trailer as a dressing room and a catering service for your meals," said Coghlan. "At Republic, you dressed where you could, had a box lunch and fought off the ants. Still, it was fun being at Republic." *(53)*

Fifty years later, Coghlan said he was still identified with that role more than any other in his long Hollywood career. He also has the same fond memories of working with Tyler that other actors and actresses had expressed through the years.

"Tom was a very close friend of my family," said Frank. "When he was making those cowboy pictures with little Frankie Darro, the director was Robert de Lacey and Mrs. De Lacey was my mother's best friend. Tom used to come over to our house for dinner quite regularly. He was a nice guy. Very shy. Very polite. I liked him a lot." *(54)*

Incredibly, Coghlan first appeared on screen in 1920 at the age of three, when Tyler was still back in Hamtramck deciding what to do with his life. The young child actor was a regular in silent films by the age of ten and appeared with such Hollywood legends as Shirley Temple, Mickey Rooney, Jackie Cooper and Charlie Chaplin.

After his movie career ended, he became a naval aviator for 23 years, and saw duty in World War II. For many of those years he headed the Navy film cooperation service. He retired from the service as a lieutenant commander.

Louise Currie (Good) was just a 22-year-old actress when she was given the lead female role of Bettie Wallace in the serial. She is on camera quite a bit during the twelve chapters, but seldom at the same time with Captain Marvel.

"We worked very fast with little or no time for retakes," she said. "Therefore, every actor was required to know his lines perfectly, and be willing to work from early morning until late at night. The situations were exciting. I didn't do much except be a victim on most of the cliffhangers.

"Tom Tyler was a wonderful, but quiet man.... a nice fellow, attractive, a good person, but was he shy! Frank Coghlan, Jr., Billy Benedict and I had lots of fun together, but Tom never seemed to join us in our good times. We chatted, laughed and enjoyed working together. Tom stayed by himself, but again, he couldn't have been nicer.

"He was very cooperative and kind," she added. "I think they (Republic) were lucky in having him as Captain Marvel because that was a kind of tricky thing to do and he did it extremely well.

"Dave Sharpe did some of the doubling for me because he was not such a tall man and was very, very good at almost anything they asked him to do. Captain Marvel was very strenuous because you are not only working fast, but the pace continues week after week. Westerns were made fast too; however, they were completed in ten days or so, and you never got quite so tired." *(55)*

When contacted in 2003, some six decades after the filming, for her recollections about Tyler, she reconfirmed statements made earlier.

"She said she really didn't know him or even anything about him, other than he was very nice, very professional and courteous," said a spokesperson for Good. "She mentioned that really they only did the quick scenes together and she never got the chance to communicate with him." *(56)*

After the success of the "Adventures of Captain Marvel" serial the rift between Captain Marvel and Superman only intensified. Seven years later, in 1948, Columbia finally made a successful serial with Kirk Alyn playing Superman. But National Comics still wanted to stop the Big Red Cheese (as Captain Marvel was known in some circles) from flying so high, at least in the comics if not on the screen.

"National gathered more evidence, enough to reopen the suit," wrote E. Nelson Birdwell in the 1977 book, *Shazam; from the '40s to the '70s.* "At first, Fawcett began digging for counter-evidence. But suddenly, Fawcett stopped building its defense.

"They had made its decision to drop their comic line and it seemed absurd to go to court to defend a character they wouldn't be publishing. So, Fawcett settled out of court, paying a large sum to National and agreeing not to publish the character without DC's consent." *(57)*

Fawcett felt the age of the superhero was coming to an end and was no longer interested in continuing its line of comics – which had grown to include more Marvel characters, such as Captain Marvel Junior, Mary Marvel, the Marvel Family and even Marvel Bunny. National (which had become DC) had won the battle.

Ironically, the Captain Marvel character resurfaced for a short comic book run in the 1970s under the DC imprint! There was also a live-action television kids program called "Shazam" and a brief animated series.

In another twist, actors playing Captain Marvel and Superman were in the same movie, back in 1939. George Reeves had the role of Brent Tarleton, one of two twins who were suitors for the hand of Scarlett O'Hara, played by Vivian Leigh, in "Gone With the Wind." From 1951 through 1957, Reeves played the title role in the "Adventures of Superman" television series.

The Captain Marvel serial was re-released several times at small movie houses in the 1960s and '70s. By the late 1990s, it was readily available through web sites and specialty video firms, complete with attractive display boxes. An entire new generation of fans could revel in the exploits of Captain Marvel, as portrayed by Tom Tyler.

The long-term popularity of the serial has surprised everyone involved with it, including Coghlan.

"When I worked on *The Adventures of Captain Marvel*, I just thought of it as another of the now more than 400 screen appearances I have made," he told P.C. Hamerlinck in a 1996 interview. "Though I starred in silent and talking feature films and many comedy short subjects, most of my fans now consider this serial to be the most important and my best-remembered work."

He recalled that during his navy days, he "would be in a chow line or walking around somewhere, and somebody would call out 'Shazam!' I always got a kick out of that."

When he was a contestant on Wheel of Fortune, he was a winner. Pat Sajak, the host, stood beside him and said, "Shazam!" *(58)*

One of the original Captain Marvel costumes from the serial has been seen on display from time to time. It was made in shades of gray so it could be filmed better in the black and white film. As late as 2003, it was listed for sale for a mere $10,000. No doubt, Tom Tyler would have been amazed.

Tarzan no, Phantom yes

E ven the success of Captain Marvel didn't mean producers were beating a path to Tyler's door to flood him with offers. After all, it was still a serial, and his stock did-n't rise much at all. In 1942, he had a small part as a strikebreaker in "The Talk of the Town," a comedy starring Cary Grant, Jean Arthur and Ronald Coleman. Ironically, Jean Arthur had been his female lead in two of Tom's westerns in 1926, "Born to Battle" and "Cowboy Cop." Three years older than Tom, she was born in Platsburgh, New York, just down the road from his hometown. She earned lasting western film fame with her role of Joe Starrett's wife, Marian, in the classic 1953 western "Shane," starring Alan Ladd and Van Heflin.

But he received another starring shot when he was offered the role of Stony Brooke in the very popular Three Mesquiteers series.

The series began in 1935 and lasted for seventeen years. A total of 51 films were made, with nine different sets of actors playing the three main roles. The first film by Republic was called "Pals of the Saddle" starring Robert Livingston, Ray Corrigan, and Max Terhune. Livingston was the star and had the role of Stony Brooke. But he left the series in 1938 and was replaced by John Wayne, who appeared in eight of the films over the next two years. Previously, Wayne had been starring in a series of low-budget westerns for Lone Star and Monogram.

In 1941, Tyler joined the series, in its eighth variation of actors in the lead roles. Although he was cast in the Livingston-Wayne role of Stony Brooke, the top billing went to Bob Steele as Tucson Smith. The third member of the trio was a comic sidekick, Rufe Davis, playing Lullaby Joslin. Their first film was "Outlaws of the Cherokee Trail," which was released late in the year.

Unlike some B stars, Tyler never was identified with a single horse, like Tom Mix's Tony or Ken Maynard's Tarzan. But, in the Three Mesquiteers series, he rode the same white horse that had been used in the 1938 and 1939 Lone Ranger serials. The horse was later ridden by Sunset Carson, another B star of the 1940s.

In his starring westerns, Tyler rode at least seven different horses, with such names as Lightning, Ace, Baron, Red, Pal and Boy. A pressbook article about "Mystery Ranch," describes Boy's intelligence and talks about the animal performing a daring act in the film. Boy was also ridden in at least two more films by Tyler, including "Terror of the Plains," and "Silver Bullet," made in 1935.

In the early 1940s, Tom was still handsome and marketable, but he wasn't a demanding star as far as the salary went, or working conditions, either. Much of the blame for his stalled career has to rest with those who were representing him – in 1941 it was the Paul Wilkins Agency on Sunset Boulevard. If they were aggressively representing him, it was-n't being reflected either in the quality of the roles he was getting or the money. He report-edly signed a standard player's contract with Republic for a year (July 8, 1941, through

July 7, 1942) for a mere $150.00 a week for the first year, and $200 for the second year. As a point of reference, that second figure was about one-hundredth of what Tom Mix reportedly was making two decades earlier as the top cowboy star in the world! However, it was the same amount that the King of the Cowboys was making in 1941.

"People assume that dad always made a lot of money in the movies, but it wasn't so," said Roy Rogers Jr. during a show at the Roy Rogers and Dale Evans Museum in Branson, Missouri, in September of 2004. "When dad started out in pictures in 1937, it was the era of the studios and contract players. He signed a contract for $150 a week and that's what he made for many years."

Long after his retirement from films, Rogers told a reporter for "Hollywood Studio Magazine" what it was like in his early years as the top western movie star in the world. "I started starving in pictures in January, 1937, for $75 a week. I was No. 1 box office before I was making $300 a week. For the first three years, my fan mail was costing me more money than I was making. I had to go on the road and beat the brush, playing one-night stands throughout the Southwest, playing these little theaters." *(59)*

Rogers said he felt an obligation to answer all the fan mail, even when he was getting 20,000 letters a week. He had to hire four girls to handle the onslaught.

The Steele-Tyler-Davis trio made seven films together, one of the last being "The Phantom Plainsmen." In the movie, Tyler has more dialogue than Steele, while Steele handles most of the fisticuffs. The film was made by Republic, the same studio that had produced "Adventures of Captain Marvel," and the scriptwriter was obviously having a bit of fun when he named one of the main characters, an older man, Captain Marvin. At the end of the film, there is a strong message for the American audience; Germany is compared to a rattlesnake and the audience was implored to support the war effort.

Starting with "Shadows on the Sage," in mid 1942, Ruffe Davis was replaced by Jimmie Dodd for six more films. The very last film in the series, number 51, was called "Riders of the Rio Grande" and it was released in May of 1943, while America was deep into World War II. Republic felt the series had run its course and made the decision to spend its efforts in promoting films with single stars like Roy Rogers and Wild Bill Elliott. In fact, Tyler's first role after completing the Stony Brooke role came at the end of 1943 in the Bill Elliott feature, "Wagon Trains West." Tyler played an Indian medicine man named Clawtooth in a small part.

But near the start of 1943 Tom received his chance to play another comic book star. Columbia Studios was looking for an actor to portray the Phantom in their fifteen-part serial based on the popular comic strip hero, and Tyler won the role. It was a bit of satisfaction for having lost out on the role of another jungle hero twelve years earlier.

In 1931, Tom was tested for the role of Tarzan but for some inexplicable reason, was not chosen. Instead, director William Wyler chose first Herman Brix and then, secondly, Johnny Weissmuller.

Tom would have been just twenty-eight years of age in 1931 when Wyler was searching for a new Apeman. Created by author Edgar Rice Burroughs, Tarzan debuted in 1912 in "All-Story Magazine." He was first played on screen in 1918 by husky Elmo Lincoln. Frank Merrill, a former gymnastics star, was the sixth actor to play Tarzan and made two movies, in 1929 and 1930, which were highly successful. A third film was planned, but the producers decided Frank did not have a voice suitable for talking pictures, which were coming on strong.

MGM secured the rights for two Tarzan films in 1930 and announced it was going to make "the biggest, most colossal jungle epic seen to date." The studio's commitment was underscored by the fact that it attached its top director, William S. Van Dyke, to the project.

"The most important thing is that he have a good physique. I want someone like Jack Dempsey, only younger," proclaimed Van Dyke. "Tom Tyler is the best so far but he is not muscular enough." *(60)*

Herman Brix, one of the very best of the twenty-one actors to play Tarzan, felt Tyler would have made a superb Tarzan. But Van Dyke wanted Brix for the role. When Brix fell and broke his shoulder while playing a small part in a movie called "Touchdown," he was sidelined for an indefinite period of time. Van Dyke decided he could not wait for Brix to heal and settled on his second choice, swimmer Johnny Weissmuller.

The film, "Tarzan The Apeman," became a huge hit and grossed over a million dollars, a watershed mark for that time. Both Weissmuller and his Jane, young and beautiful Maureen O'Sullivan, became major stars as a result of the film's success. Weissmuller eventually played the role in twelve films, spanning a total of seventeen years.

Ironically, Brix was given a second shot at playing Tarzan when an independent film company acquired the rights from Burroughs to make a pair of Tarzan films. Those two 1930s movies, "The New Adventures of Tarzan" and "Tarzan and the Green Goddess," made Brix the most admired of all film Tarzans in the opinion of many of the genre's experts.

While Weissmuller did a superb job of portraying the savage jungle man in his debut, it's hard to understand why Van Dyke preferred him to Tyler. From years of dedicated weight training, Tyler had a much more impressive physique than Weissmuller, who always looked rather smooth from a muscular standpoint.

The Phantom was, like Tarzan, an extremely powerful character who lived in the wilds (of Bengali, not Africa) but, unlike Tarzan, he did not go about his duties attired only in a flimsy loincloth. The Phantom was decked out in a skin-tight purple outfit complete with heavy black boots and a black mask. Instead of a hunting knife at his side, he wore a pair of revolvers.

The Phantom comic strip debuted on February 17, 1936, and he was the first such hero to fight crime while wearing a costume and hiding his true identity. Lee Falk created the strip and reportedly drew on tales of Zorro and The Scarlet Pimpernel for his inspiration. Falk did the writing while a series of talented artists handled the artwork through the years.

"I tried to think up a more original title," said Falk. "There was already The Phantom of the Opera, the phantom of this and the phantom of that. For a while I considered calling him The Gray Ghost but I let it ride because I really couldn't come up with a title I liked better than The Phantom.

"The Phantom comes out of my great interest as a kid in hero stories, the great myths and legends – Greek, Roman, Scandinavian, the Songs of Roland, El Cid in Spain, King Arthur and others. There's a heroic thing about him, he's sort of a legendary character. He started out fairly simple and gradually I've added more and more legendary things about him till he has a whole folklore around him.

"*The Jungle Book* of Kipling's and *Tarzan of the Apes* influenced me, as you can imagine. Apparently, this legendary quality seems to be the most popular feature of The

Phantom with readers." *(61)*

The Phantom of 1943, named Godfrey Prescott in the serial, was the 21st in a line which stretched back over 400 years. Each Phantom would train his son to take over when the time came, and he became known as "The Ghost Who Walks" because he seemed to never age, or die. Only his loyal Bantu warriors knew the real secret of his identity and succession. The storyline was a familiar one – revolving around a lost city (called Zoloz) and, of course, a hidden treasure.

"When the movies finally got around to The Phantom, they did him justice with a fine action star, Tom Tyler," wrote the authors of *The Great Movie Serials.* "At that time, he was noted primarily for Westerns, but he projected such a quality of unmistakable hero-ism (that) he proved well-suited to play a larger-than-life costumed hero. Though he is sometimes accused of being 'wooden'; in speech and movements, he might well be described as the Gary Cooper of the serials." *(62)*

Tyler looked very impressive in the Phantom suit. At age forty, he was still lean and muscular, and moved easily in the action scenes. Once again, he was considered an ideal choice for a larger-than-life role. Not only did he have the perfect physique, but he simply looked heroic and pulled off the role with ease, just as he had with Captain Marvel.

If Vincent Markowski was born to be a hero, then Tom Tyler was the person that could make it happen.

"It was generally agreed that no other actor could have resembled the main character more than Tom Tyler," wrote an author in *The Big Reel* publication in 1996. "Dressed up in the form-fitting outfit topped by the cowl and mask of Falk's mystery hero, he was the Phantom. In that regard, he even surpassed his portrayal of Captain Marvel, although there was comparisons between the two serials. The Phantom stands in the company of the best serials Columbia Pictures made, in whose place it would be very hard to place any other person." *(63)*

"Unquestionably, The Phantom was one of Columbia's better serials, although beginning to show that studio's notorious low budget defects," said the authors of *The Great Movie Serials. (64)*

In reality, the serial almost looks like it was two different films, the first half being good enough to pass the test and the second half somewhat weaker. A fight with a gorilla named Brutus in chapter twelve is as ludicrous a "battle" as has ever been seen on a movie screen. The Phantom walks into a pit and finds himself face to face with the beast. They wrestle briefly and then the gorilla winds up on the floor of the pit, with the Phantom lean-ing over him, hands on his face, pulling his jaws apart. Soft, soothing music that would be more appropriate for a festive dinner plays in the background as the two struggle. The strange maneuver somehow manages to kill the beast and the Phantom emerges unscathed.

There are plenty of fights in the 15 chapters and the Phantom, with his faithful dog Devil at his side, is suitably heroic. The chapters are entitled as follows: 1 - The Sign of the Skull, 2 - The Man Who Never Dies, 3 - A Traitor's Code, 4 - The Seat of Judgement, 5 - The Ghost Who Walks, 6 - Jungle Whispers, 7 - The Mystery Well, 8 - In Quest of The Keys, 9 - The Fire Princess, 10 - The Chamber of Death, 11 - The Emerald Key, 12 - The Fangs of the Beast, 13 - The Road to Zoloz, 14 - The Lost City, and 15 - Peace in The Jungle.

As popular as the Phantom serial was with the youth of America, it was still a serial and again did little to help Tyler get more meaningful roles. He continued on in his Three Mesquiteers series. A promotional sheet for "Westward Ho" ran short bios of the three stars, as well as the female lead, Evelyn Brand. It provided some very interesting information about Tom's personal life, including that he liked to fly, was interested in cooking…. and that he was still married.

"Born into a thrifty immigrant family, Tom Tyler's success is shining proof of the opportunities offered by America to her sons, both native and adopted," began the promotional piece. "Tom's father came to this country a humble immigrant from his native Lithuania, but lived to attain a position of importance in the iron mines near Port Henry, New York, where he settled.

"And his son, Tom, who started out as a water boy in the mines, is now one of the screen's most popular action heroes…"

Later on, it mentioned that Tom was "an enthusiastic aviator and has over sixty hours in the air to his credit. He is an expert cook and likes to putter around in the kitchen. Sirloin tips are his specialty. Tom has been in business twice, once in a real estate venture and again as silent partner in a tile manufacturing concern, but he now devotes all his time to acting."

It also mentioned that Tom was "happily married to Jeanne Martel, an actress, and they live in a Spanish-style hillside home. In the basement of this home is a workshop where he indulges his hobby of cabinet making."

But the "happily married" line was almost certainly an exaggeration. After five years of marriage, Tom and Jeanne divorced and went their separate ways. It was a fate that befell many of the film stars of the era. At best, marriage was a shaky institution in the fast lane of Hollywood, and there were several reasons for it, according to author Leventhal:

> It is true that the divorce and remarriage rate in Hollywood was far higher than the rest of the nation. No doubt part of the reason stemmed from the fact that Hollywood contained more handsome men and sexy females than any other city in the world.

> There was another reason, as well: the murderous work schedules. Shooting often began at dawn and lasted until after nightfall. Often a movie husband and wife, working on different locations, wouldn't see each other for weeks on end. As they worked in an ever-increasing atmosphere of pressure, it is not hard to understand the fate that overcame (some of them). Or why actors and actresses married and married and married and married.

> This then was Hollywood in the '30s, a town filled with beautiful and too often semi literate men and women who suddenly found themselves famous. A town with uncounted thousands of call girls who commanded up to $1,000 a night.

> It was a town of phonies and down-to-earth people, of seekers of the fast buck and of dedicated artists, of sleek limousines and of tattered jalopies, of sleazy one-room apartments climbing the steep slopes of Hollywood and of

fabulous mansions. It was filled with dreamers of dreams of stardom that would never come true.

In short, post-Depression Hollywood was utterly unlike any other sleepy town in the world that suddenly found itself a mini-metropolis. With the coming of the war years, it retained some of its kookiness but it was never again quite the way it was in the '30s. (65)

The marriage of Tom Tyler and Jeanne Martel was apparently one of the casualties of the blazing and demanding lifestyle. They had gotten married in a rush after a whirlwind courtship by Tom. For whatever reasons, they simply could not make a go of it. No living members of the Tyler extended family know what happened, and dismiss the divorce with a shrug, as if to say "such things happen in life." Mike Tyler, the son of Frank, Jr., says he heard a rumor that Jeanne simply ran off with another man after Tom's illness became apparent. It was the same story that Ray Slepski had been told by his mother, Katherine.

There was another actress in Hollywood at the time named June Martel, who appeared with Buster Crabbe in the film, "Arizona Mahoney," made by Paramount in 1936. Some researchers have suggested she was a sister to Jeanne, but there is no evidence of that. If so, they weren't very close, as June is not listed among the guests at Jeanne's wedding, and there is no mention of Jeanne in the short marriage write-up between June Martel and Frank Fenton, a Hollywood writer, in 1941.

Jeanne appeared in just six movies, the last one "Bringing Up Baby" in 1938, where she has a brief, non-speaking role. June Martel was in 11 films, the last one also coming in 1938. Whatever their relationship, if any, both of the Martel women seem to have disappeared from the Hollywood scene shortly after Jeanne's marriage to Tom dissolved, and they left no trail at all after 1938.

In the early 1940s, Tom was staying fairly busy with his Mesquiteer work. Of the 12 main actors to have played in the series, Livingston led the way with 29 films, followed by Ray "Crash" Corrigan with 24, Max Tehrune with 21 and Steele with 20. Tyler was in sixth place with 13 to his credit.

With the release of the last film, the three Mesquiteers were left to fend for themselves. Tyler's contract expired in July of 1943 and he was basically out on the street, searching for work anywhere he could find it. Steele quickly moved on to other western companies and was able to stay busy in the profession. Davis and Dodd kicked around Hollywood for a decade or more and they, with Steele, all wound up on solid television programs. Dodd eventually became one of the hosts of the Mickey Mouse Club Show, which was very popular in the 1950s, while Davis had a regular role on "Petticoat Junction." Steele appeared in several episodes of "Gunsmoke" and other TV westerns and finally landed a regular role on "F Troop" in the 1960s.

The era of the great cowboy stars was over. Mix had died in 1940, and near the end of 1942 the genre lost another of its legends when Buck Jones died tragically. Jones was among over four hundred victims that perished in the aftermath of the Coconut Grove nightclub fire on November 28 in Boston. Jones was just fifty-three years old at the time of his passing.

Tom Tyler was still alive and in good health, but after the Mesquiteers series his starring days were over and the remaining seven years of the 1940s were not very productive for him. He was in six films in 1943, and seven in 1944. He started out in 1944 with second billing to Rod Cameron in "Boss of Boomtown" and was in three non-westerns, entitled "Ladies of Washington," "The Navy Way" and "The Princess and the Pirate."

There are just three film credits in 1945, two in 1946 and a single film in 1947. One can imagine that whatever savings he might have had were quickly used up when his steady paychecks disappeared. But his work schedule improved in 1948 with six films, including "Red River" with John Wayne, Montgomery Clift and Walter Brennan. Tyler is a cowhand seen in the background in the first hour of the film, and is one of three men who challenge Wayne's character, the trail boss. Shots are fired, and all three of the rebels are killed. It's not obvious if Wayne got Tyler again, as in "Stagecoach," or if Clift does him in.

In 1949, Tyler had roles in another Wayne film, "She Wore a Yellow Ribbon," directed by John Ford, and in the biblical epic, "Samson and Delilah," starring Victor Mature and Hedy Lamar. They were just tiny parts, but Tyler apparently had some reason to remember the scene in the Biblical tale. He told his nephew, Ray Slepski, that Delilah (Lamar) said he came to close to her in the scene he had with her.

The role in "She Wore a Yellow Ribbon" was quite memorable for more aesthetic reasons. It was strong enough that it has been singled out for comment by film writers on several occasions.

"Purists, especially lovers of John Ford films, are most impressed by the storm scene, particularly in a sequence in which a cavalry doctor (Arthur Shields) is operating on a soldier (Tom Tyler) inside a moving wagon train," wrote one film critic. ""What makes the scene special is that much of the sequence was filmed in the dark with only flashes of lighting to illustrate the camera." *(66)*

However brilliant, such scenes meant only a couple of days of work and little more. All in all, he was in nine films in 1949 and eleven in 1950.

In 1950, he was being used mostly as second-string villains in films with the "new" cowboy heroes, men like Whip Wilson ("Outlaws of Texas") and Lash LaRue ("King of the Bullwhip"). He was also was one of eight major cowboy stars that had cameo roles in the Roy Rogers hit, "Trail of Robin Hood." The plot revolved around efforts by retired movie star Jack Holt to harvest evergreens to sell as Christmas trees and donate the proceeds to needy children. The film was directed by William Witney, who had directed Tyler in "The Adventures of Captain Marvel." It is not hard to imagine that Witney arranged for the fading star to get at least one more small payday.

Near the end of the film, the stars begin riding up as Roy is about to engage a villain in a gunfight. First comes Rocky Lane, followed by Monte Hale, Bill Farnum and Crash Corrigan. Then three stars – Kermit Maynard, Tom Keene and Tom Tyler – arrive at the same time, and Rocky Lane introduces them to Roy.

"Roy, you remember Tom Tyler," says Lane as Tom dismounts and shakes hands with the King of the Cowboys. Tyler is wearing a brown shirt trimmed in white at the top and a white hat. Long gone is the hard, lean look and the all-black outfit that made him such a standout in the late 1920s and early 1930s.

"Hi, Roy, we hear there's a fight going on," says Tom in his familiar voice.

George Cheesboro, a veteran bad guy, arrives and, finally, Rex Allen, the last of the singing cowboys. All of the western heroes wind up steering wagons full of trees, racing across a burning bridge while Roy slugs it out with two villains under the bridge.

"Tom was a real gentleman and a very nice guy to work with," said Monte Hale in 2004, fifty-four years after the fact. "We didn't get to spend much time together, but it was a pleasure to be in the film with him." *(67)*

In his brief appearance it is not yet obvious that Tyler is showing the effects of the disease that would soon cripple him and take his life just four short years later. But in the movie "Fast On the Draw," released later in 1950, he is seen hiding behind the bar in a fight scene, and his face looks drawn and tight, symptoms of the disease. The film starred Jimmy Ellison and Russell Hayden, and Tyler was listed behind other character actors Fuzzy Knight, Raymond Hatton, Betty Adams and George Lewis. It is apparent that a long and outstanding career is riding up to its final horizon.

There were still a few film efforts left for Tom, including two in 1951 and five in 1952. His last movie was "Cow Country," made by Allied Artists and released in 1953. It was directed by Lesley Selander, who had begun making films with Buck Jones two decades earlier, and featured Edmond O'Brien, Raymond Hatton, Peggie Castle, Robert Lowery and Lane Chandler.

But the era of the B western was drawing to a close. The genre had enjoyed a long run, but after World War II things were different in Hollywood and America. Most of the stars of Tyler's era had either died or were too old to keep playing hero roles and the new breed of western stars – Lash LaRue, Whip Wilson, Jim Bannon (as Red Ryder) and Eddie Dean – were not strong enough to excite the audiences in the same manner as had Mix, Jones, Gibson, Maynard and Tyler. In addition, television was producing western shows like "The Adventures of Wild Bill Hickok" and "Hopalong Cassidy," and was filling the gap. Even Roy Rogers and Gene Autry made the move to TV eventually, and the B western was finished at the movie theater. All that remained were the classier westerns of such stars as Randolph Scott, Joel McCrea and, of course, John Wayne.

Tyler supplemented his movie income in the early 1950s with television work, landing small roles in a number of programs, including "The Lone Ranger," "The Gene Autry Show," "Roy Rogers," "The Adventures of Wild Bill Hickock," "Cisco Kid" and even "Sky King."

In late 1952 he was involved in a project that the producers, a company called The Tucson Kid Productions, hoped would lead to a television series. A pilot was made called "Crossroad Avenger – The Adventures of the Tucson Kid." It featured Tom Keene as a western insurance agent called the Tucson Kid, and Tyler as a deputy. Character actor Lyle Talbot was the main bad guy. The infamous Ed Wood wrote the story and directed the pilot.

The pilot was shot in full color, which was unusual for that time period, but was very weak in story line, acting and direction. It did not sell to a network and just the one episode was made. Unfortunately, Tyler would not have been able to work much longer even if the pilot had caught on and become a series. Tragedy was lurking in the shadows, about to render the once powerful figure a crushing blow.

Tyler was capable of and willing to play villains as well as heroes. In 1939, he played Luke Plummer (right), the foe of John Wayne in "Stagecoach" and in 1940 he played the loathsome Mummy (bottom) in "The Mummy's Hand."

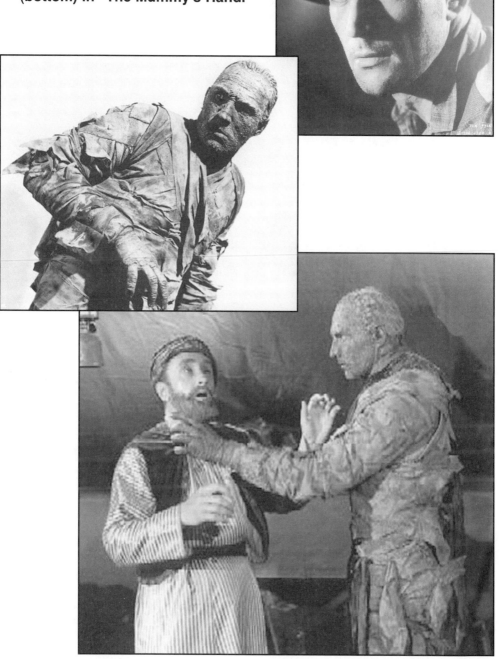

In 1941, Tom was given the lead role in the exciting serial, "The Adventures of Captain Marvel." It is still considered the best serial ever made, and Tom's portrayal of the superhero is one of the main reasons.

LEFT: Tom towers over Gene Autry and a Republic executive when they meet on the Republic lot during a break in the filming of Captain Marvel.

BOTTOM: Tom meets Gene again, this time when the nation's top cowboy star is astride Champion.

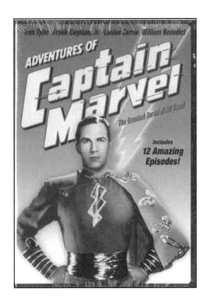

TOP: The 1941 serial is still a popular item as a video in 2005.

RIGHT: Captain Marvel has his muscles tested by comedian Judy Canova.

Captain Marvel has no problem holding off two villains after he arrives on the scene in Siam. Captain Marvel comics actually outsold Superman comics in the early 1940s.

Tom Tyler gets a chance to show off his weightlifting power during a scene from the serial, "The Adventures of Captain Marvel." The former national weightlifting champion was a perfect choice to play the comic-book hero, for both his personal appearance and acting abilities.

(Captain Marvel is a trademark character owned by DC Comics)

RIGHT: Young Louise Good had to be saved by the mighty Captain.

BELOW: Even facially, Tom Tyler looked a great deal like the comic-book hero.

RIGHT: This villain (played by veteran actor Keane Duncan) is in big trouble.

Tyler was paid a mere $250 a week for his starring role in the 12-chapter production, still considered one of the best serials ever made.

Tom Tyler cut
a dashing figure
as the mysterious
Phantom and
made the comic-
book hero spring
to life in the
popular serial.

BOTTOM: As the new and coming Phantom, Tom Tyler (left) stood by his dying father, the old Phantom, in the opening chapter of the 1943 serial made by Columbia Studios.

(The Phantom is a trademark character of King Features Syndicate.)

LEFT: The Phantom dangles from a rope ladder during a perilous moment in the serial. Tyler was in top shape for the role and looked terrific in the skin-tight uniform of The Ghost Who Walks.

BOTTOM: Jeanne Bates had the lead female role in the serial. She was just 22 years old at the time of the filming, in 1943.

LEFT: In 1941, Tom (left) took over the role of Stoney Brooke in the popular series, "3 Mesquiteers." He made seven films with co-stars Ruff Davis (center) and Bob Steele.

RIGHT: Jimmie Dodd (center) took over for Ruff Davis in the final six films in the series.

LEFT: In the film "Shadows on the Sage," the three pals even tried singing, briefly.

ABOVE: Tom Tyler was an impressive Indian warrior Geronimo in the 1942 film, "Valley of the Sun," produced by RKO Studios. It was one of nine movies Tom appeared in that year. Seven of them were westerns, but he also was in "The Mummy's Tomb" and a Cary Grant film called "The Talk of the Town."

RIGHT: Long before she became TV's queen of comedy, Lucille Ball was playing in a western called "Valley of the Sun" with Tyler.

Members of the Markowski clan visited Tom's home in Beverly Hills and posed for this photo. They are (from left) Tom's mother, Helen; a friend, Viola, and Tom's father, Frank Markowski, Sr.

(Photo courtesy of Mike Tyler)

TOP: Family members visited Tom in California on several occasions. Here sisters Mollie (left) and Katherine and brother Frank pose with their famous sibling.

LEFT: Frank holds his young son Mike with his mother and Tom at his side.

(Photos courtesy of Mike Tyler)

In "Badman's Territory," the 1946 film made by RKO, Tyler played Frank James, the brother of the notorious outlaw, Jesse James. Randolph Scott, Ann Richards and Gabby Hayes were the primary stars.

One of Tom's last efforts was the 1950 Roy Rogers film, "Trail of Robin Hood," made by Republic Pictures. Tom and other cowboy stars show up in the closing minutes to help Roy thwart the bad guys and deliver Christmas trees. The stars were (back row, from left), Rex Allen, Tom Tyler, Ray "Crash" Corrigan, Allan "Rocky" Lane, Monte Hale, George Cheesboro, Kermit Maynard, (front row, from left) Tom Keene, Roy Rogers, William Farnum and Jack Holt.

LEFT: Nearly crippled by scleroderma, Tom returned to the Detroit area to live with the family of his sister, Katherine Slepski. Tom liked to sit on the front porch and watch the neighbors passing by.

RIGHT: Tom was near the end of his life when this photo was taken in the Slepski home.

LEFT: Tom Tyler rests in Mt. Olivet Cemetery in Detroit. He died on May 4, 1954, and hundreds of fans came from around the country on very short notice to pay their respects.

(All photos on this page courtesy of the Ray Slepski family.)

TOM TYLER
1903 — 1954

Back to Michigan

Vincent Markowski was nothing if not resilient. Even when his friend, Emil Karkoski, turned back in Denver on their journey to California in 1923, Vincent was not to be denied and finished the trip by himself. Working the studios looking for any type of a break, he was able to parlay his tremendous physique and good looks into an opportunity to get on screen.

When sound came, he made the transition with ease while others fell by the wayside. When the singing cowboy craze emerged, he still managed to survive by becoming a sought-after character actor, and by working in serials.

Tyler could have been a much bigger star than he was, in the opinion of many. He had everything that it took, including the desire to work long and hard to improve himself. What he apparently lacked the most was an astute agent to guide him to the best parts and to make sure he was on the "A list" of persons who were making the decisions.

"It would be the blight of Tom Tyler's career, in one opinion, that he never received the care and attention he needed, and deserved, to become a top-ranking cowboy star," said Don Miller in his book, *Hollywood Corral*. "Tyler was unique, but his strongest qualities were not so immediately apparent, and ran deeper. He was imposing in appearance. His acting was restrained, and more than satisfactory, even in the desperate inept situations, and he would have more than his share of them.

"The intriguing thing about Tyler was his somewhat sinister attitude, underlined by piercing eyes and deep but repressed speaking voice, as if the sounds were coming from the shadows. More than any other range hero, Tyler gave the impression of tensile, quiet menace – that if he were on the prowl for an adversary, that bad one's fate would not be a pleasant one to watch." *(68)*

Tom Tyler was able to overcome weak scripts and poor production values during his long career, and just kept plugging along with the same work ethic his father had displayed decades earlier in both Port Henry and Hamtramck. But one problem he was not able to overcome was a terrible illness known as scleroderma. It was a frightening disease that began to creep into his body in the late 1940s. Eventually, it forced him into smaller and smaller roles as the disease severely crippled his magnificent body. It even changed his facial features to the extent that he no longer looked like the same man. In the Tucson Kid pilot, Tyler is stiff and wooden in the few action scenes and his face appears drawn and tight. With the drastic physical changes and the limitations on his movements, Tyler's abilities also faded, and so did his marketability.

"You're never really big in Hollywood," wrote Mickey Rooney in his autobiography. "You're only as big as your last picture or series. And above all, the cardinal sin is being broke. The hands that will help you are few while the hands that will help themselves are many." *(69)*

What Mickey Rooney writes about in his autobiography is a sad fact of life in the film world, with few exceptions. Once the top-rated movie star in the world as a young-ster, Rooney was a long time between jobs just a decade later. Hollywood may seem excit-ing and lucrative to all those outside, but inside there are long periods of inactivity and the constant, gnawing threat that each film may be your last.

Tom Tyler, once one of the most handsome men in Hollywood and certainly in the 1930s the most physically powerful of all actors, experienced what Rooney would write about years later. By the end of 1952, with little money saved or coming in and harboring scant hope of any future film opportunities, Tyler's opportunities in the film business were nearly exhausted. Scleroderma accomplished what the coming of sound and the emer-gence of singing cowboys could not: It ended his career.

So what was this terrible disease and how did it attack a person as powerful and out-wardly healthy as Tom Tyler? The name comes from two Greek words: 'sclera' and 'derma' mean 'hard skin.' Even a casual observer can notice the skin changes of people who have the illness. The face tightens and often shines, and even smiling is difficult. Finger and hand skin can become so taut that a person can lose the ability to grip a fork or a pencil.

"Scleroderma can involve internal organs," says a brochure from the Scleroderma Foundation in Byfield, Massachusetts. "The same process going on in the skin can enmesh the lungs in strands of scar tissue so dense that the victim struggles for air. Scar tissue in the esophagus makes swallowing painful and troublesome. In the digestive tract it inhibits the absorption of nutrients. Joints all over the body might throb with pain. Kidney involve-ment is particularly treacherous. It leads to high blood pressure and kidney failure."

The cause is unknown. According to the Scleroderma Foundation, "the evidence suggests that the susceptible host for scleroderma is someone with a genetic predisposi-tion to injure from an environmental insult. This insult either directly causes injury to blood vessels or indirectly perturbs the blood vessels by activating the immune system."

Following is information from a fact sheet offered by the Foundation:

- Scleroderma is an autoimmune disease whose symptoms typically include some or all of the following: sensitivity to cold in fingers and hands, thickening of the skin, shortness of breath, difficulty swallowing, joint stiffness and pain, and dam-age to internal organs.

- Autoimmune diseases, which affect more than 50 million Americans, are the third leading cause of death in the United States.

- There are an estimated 300,000 cases of scleroderma in the United States.

- 80 percent of patients are female.

- Scleroderma typically strikes between the ages of 25 and 55.

- 95 percent of scleroderma cases begin with Raynaud's phenomenon (hands and feet abnormally sensitive to cold).

- Federal research funding for scleroderma lags behind other diseases of similar prevalence.

- In 2003, the Scleroderma Foundation granted $1.2 million in research grants to the medical community.

- Misdiagnosis is common. It can take three years or more for an individual to be diagnosed and receive appropriate treatment, often due to lack of familiarity with the disease among medical professionals.

With his career in tatters due to the illness, Tom had few resources in California to fall back upon. Gene Autry, who had posed for photos with Tom during his Captain Marvel days, was one of the few who knew of Tom's situation and tried to help out.

"I had the extreme good fortune to work with Tom in two 'Gene Autry' TV shows," said veteran actor Bill Kennedy. "We all knew that Tom was terminal and that Gene had hired him as a tribute. We loved Gene for this gesture. Tom gave a superlative performance in both segments. We spent a week with Tom and I got to talk to him about his fascinating career. He knew Doug Fairbanks, Valentino, John Gilbert, Tom Mix, William S. Hart, Chaplain.

"John Ford liked him, as well as many other famous directors of that time. As a result of the Autry stints, Tom had enough money to go back to Hamtramck in style, to his sister's house, where he died with dignity and respect." *(70)*

In yet another small link between the Captain Marvel and Superman characters, Kennedy had supplied the dramatic voice at the beginning of each episode of the Superman television series: "Faster than a speeding bullet, more powerful than a locomotive…"

Leaving Hollywood weak and ill, Tom sought haven in the home of his sister, Katherine Slepski, and her family. They had a lovely home in the Polish section of the northern Detroit suburb and they welcomed Vincent with open arms.

"I have several memories of Uncle Tom when he came back to live with us," said Ray Slepski in 2004. Slepski was a young boy when a sick and weary Tyler returned to live in their home at 13158 Moenart. He recalls that Tyler arrived with little more than the clothes on his back, and he remembers all too well the terrible impact the disease had on his famous uncle.

"His skin was very hard," said Slepski. "He had trouble walking. His fingers were curved and he could hardly move them. Back then, vendors used to travel the streets selling or delivering milk, vegetables, etc. I remember how Uncle Tom used to love to eat fresh corn on the cob from the vendors when it was in season, even though he struggled with his hands.

"Since Uncle Tom was such a handsome and strong man in his early years, it was hard on my mother to see him in this condition and to care for him. I think it took a terrible toll on her. But she never complained, and neither did my father. It was the ethnic thing to do back then; family took care of family, and that's all there was to it."

Young Ray gave up his upstairs bedroom to his uncle, and moved down the hall, to the bedroom in front overlooking the street. There was only one bathroom in the house and it was straight across the hallway from Tom's room. There was a small steam bath cabinet in there and Tyler used it frequently. "I think it helped with his hands and skin," Slepski said.

Tyler's favorite place to sit was in the parlor on the west side of the house, a comfortable but small room that offered a view of the large, grassy side lot and houses down the street. He would sit there by the hour, Ray recalled.

"We called it a sun porch back then. We were never allowed to sit in Uncle Tom's chair in the sun porch. That was his chair. But he did ask me to buy an old jalopy car from across the street. I was just sixteen and I went over and bought it with his money. Once when I was driving it, I ran it into the big iron gate next to the house (the gate was still there in 2004). I came in to tell him what I had done, and he just shrugged. 'It's,' he said. 'Nothing was hurt so it's okay.'

"Sometimes, he would go out and sit on the front porch and neighbors would come over and talk to him, and ask questions about Hollywood. He would tell them stories and answer their questions. I remember him saying who were the good guys and the bad guys that he worked with, but I can't recall who he was talking about, it's been so long ago. I wish I could now, of course. But he was friendly and answered all their questions."

Tom Kozyra was the son of Mollie, Tom's youngest sister. He also recalls the few meetings with his famous relative when "Uncle Tom" came to visit.

"My mother was the oldest and it was all one big, happy family in the household," recalled Kozyra. "My grandmother lived downstairs and two other couples and a tenant lived upstairs. There were Lithuanians, a Russian, a Ukranian and a Pole all living in the same house.

"We had streetcars back then and I remember once that grandma was going to take me downtown to see Santa Claus, on the streetcar. But Uncle Tom was visiting from California, and said he wouldn't allow that. He ran out and bought a new Buick, bright blue, with a white convertible top, and drove us downtown to see Santa Claus. I remember that more than seeing Santa. It was such a nice thing to do that I have never forgotten it," said Kozyra.

Ray Slepski wonders if Tyler really bought the car or rented it, or if the local car dealer loaned it to him for the short time he was in town, since no one knows what happened to the car and they don't remember Tyler driving back to Los Angeles in it.

Marilyn Beaudrie never met Tom Tyler but she knew the Slepski family well. Her sister, Joanne, wound up marrying Ray.

"It was a beautiful home," said Marilyn of the house that Tom moved into on Moenart. "It had a gorgeous chandelier in the dining room and nice woodwork. Katherine Slepski was a very friendly and outgoing person and her husband was a wonderful man. In fact, Kathryn and Tom Tyler looked alike. She had the same facial features as he did. But apparently she and Tom didn't have similar personalities, as I have heard he was shy and quiet and she was very warm and outgoing."

Joanne Slepski also remembers her mother-in-law as a "very special, gracious lady. Just so kind and wonderful to everyone."

Sandy Slepski recalls how impressed she was when Tyler came to visit when she was a very young girl. "I remember sitting on his lap and he was dressed in a beautiful suit," she said in 2004. "I remember thinking, 'Who is this guy?' Mother said, 'He's your Uncle Tom and he's a movie star.' He certainly looked like a movie star."

Sandy eventually moved to California and became a nurse. Several times she was on duty when Clayton Moore, who earned considerable fame as The Lone Ranger on television, came to the hospital for health care late in his life. He had worked with Tyler on several films.

"I mentioned to Mr. Moore that Tom Tyler was my uncle and he was very interested in that," said Sandy. "He told me, 'Out of all the people I worked with, Tom loved his work the most. Through all the ups and downs, and there were plenty of both for all actors, he never complained and was always upbeat. He just loved the work.' "

Moore's comments echoed the words of stuntman David Sharpe during the filming of Captain Marvel. Sharpe had observed Tyler being strapped into a cumbersome outfit and being suspended hours on end during the simulated flying scenes; yet Tyler had never complained once despite the great discomfort he had to be enduring.

Mike Tyler, the son of Frank, Jr., was born and raised in California and during his youth spent considerable time with his famous uncle.

"He was a very jovial and happy person," said Tyler. "He always told me he was going to teach me how to ride a horse, but we never seemed to get around to it."

One can only imagine what thoughts ran through Tom Tyler's mind during the last year of his life. In his youth, he had seemed invincible, with a physique that was envied by all and a power flowing through his body that few men anywhere in the entire world could match. He had once nurtured very lofty dreams and had the courage to chase his aspirations all the way to young Hollywood. He had conquered all he had set out to accomplish – from the world of weightlifting to the exciting world of movies.

He became the first actor to portray a superhero on screen, and then repeated that success with another superhero role. Though he never made huge money, he had been a star! He had earned the respect of his peers and was well liked by those who knew him personally, and idolized by millions who only knew him on the giant screen. And then his world collapsed in the pain and suffering of a stunning, debilitating disease that was practically unknown. He must have sat by the hour in his room in the house at 13158 Moenart and wondered how this saga had come to such an ending.

Tom's courageous battle with the disease came to a close on the morning of May 3, 1954. He was taken by ambulance to St. Francis Hospital, where he died. He was three months shy of his fifty-first birthday. According to the death certificate, the official reason was heart failure, while scleroderma was listed as an "antecedent cause."

"Cardiac involvement is a potential (and potentially deadly) complication of scleroderma," said Jackie Blint, education manager of the Scleroderma Foundation in Byfield, Massachusetts. "In addition, in the past, it was referred to as a rare form of arthritis. Scleroderma is associated with arthritis, and is also variously referred to as a connective tissue disease, a collagen vascular disease, an autoimmune disease, and a rheumatic disease."

Whatever it is called, scleroderma is a frightening and debilitating disease. That it is far more common among women than men is just another sad irony of the Tom Tyler story; it seems hard to believe that one of the most powerful men of his generation would fall prey to such a rare disease, but life is often stranger than fiction, especially in Hollywood.

Epilogue

It is possible that no actor has ever played a greater variety of characters than did Vincent Markowski, the kid from Port Henry, New York. He started out as cowboy hero Tom Tyler, having lead roles in a wide range of films geared toward the young audience of the 1920s and '30s, in the early days of moviemaking. He portrayed real-life characters such as the great scout Buffalo Bill Cody and the legendary Indian leader Geronimo. He was totally believable as the comic-book heroes Captain Marvel and the Phantom, as well as Clancy of the Mounties.

He could play any role equally well, from his stint as a scary mummy to the bad guy in "Stagecoach" and a Confederate officer in "Gone With the Wind." He rubbed shoulders with such legendary film stars as John Wayne, Cary Grant, Jean Arthur, Humphrey Bogart, Errol Flynn and Marlene Dietrich, both on and off the screen.

There seems to be another ironic twist, or dichotomy, to his life – which is that he was an introverted personality in a profession that caused one to emote constantly. There is little doubt that he was a shy man most of his life; the evidence for that is conclusive. But he was also a man of inner confidence, willing to take huge risks in his own abilities, over and over. He had the courage to strike out from Detroit as a young man in 1923 and to stay on course even when his friend turned back in Denver.

He had a tremendous work ethic, both as a result of his environment and his inner makeup. He enjoyed working hard for what he wanted – from a weight room where he crafted a sensational physique for his era, to learning the demanding craft of acting.

Maybe Vincent Markowski and the Phantom had more in common than one would guess at first blush. Tom Tyler was the alter ego of Vincent, just as Captain Marvel and the Phantom were the alter egos of Billy Batson and a man named Walker!

Tom Tyler appeared in a stunning total of 150-plus films, including both two-reelers and features, and dozens of television shows. He can be found among the most popular movies ever made and some of the most popular "B" westerns and serials of all time. His impact on the world of film was sizeable, but has been largely forgotten by all but a few diehards who study the genre of western movies and serials, and who respect his body of work.

"His tenure as a cowboy star stretched back to the silents and was long and noble," wrote film historian Don Miller. "The feeling persists that with creative and intensive guidance, the attributes of Tom Tyler, buried as they were under an avalanche of neglect and carelessness, could have been transformed into a screen image approaching the highest plateaus. That it didn't happen is too bad." *(71)*

Western author Stormy Weathers agrees with that assessment.

"The best example of a classic waste of talent might be Tom Tyler," he wrote. "He deserved a much better fate than he received. He was big, handsome and a good actor.

Tyler's career was characterized by more twists, turns and ups and downs than a roller coaster ride." *(72)*

Chuck Anderson has dedicated his wonderful web site, The Old Corral, to many "B" cowboy stars. Of course, Tom Tyler is one of the subjects. At the end, Anderson summarizes Tyler's career thusly:

> *Though he was tall, muscular, and looked downright impressive, Tom was often saddled with slipshod efforts at Syndicate, Monogram, Reliable and Victory – included were anemic production values, lack of directorial finesse, shoestring budgets and inane scripts. Tyler often appeared stiff and ill-at-ease mouthing the oftentimes-incredulous dialog. Some writers note that Tom's delivery problems were due to his Lithuanian accent, but I'm not sure that is the case. It may have just been a lack of training and experience.*

> *However, when given better material such as Captain Marvel, The Phantom, and the Mesquiteers features, Tom's overall performance was enjoyable and above par. But perhaps his real calling was gunfighter roles such as "Powdersmoke Range" and "Stagecoach," for his penetrating stare and sinister mannerisms brought instant hisses (and critical acclaim).*

> *His seven serials rival that of cliffhanger "king" Buster Crabbe. Overall, Tyler had a near thirty-year career spotted with ups and downs, trials and tribulations, mediocrity and success. Interestingly, his career and that of Bob Steele were remarkably similar. But because of fan appeal, talent, luck or whatever, Steele is remembered today along with the likes of Jones, Mix, and other big names. Yet Tom Tyler seems to have been forgotten. He deserves better for his 90-plus western starring roles represent both extremes of the B western spectrum, from the Poverty Row oaters at Freuler/Monarch, Reliable and Victory to the quality and polish of Republic. Thankfully, much of his work is still aired on cable and available on videotape.*

> *Tom Tyler was a talented workhorse who brought some real excitement to those wonderful Saturday matinees. (73)*

Tom Tyler was a young man when he rode into a young Hollywood in 1923, and he grew with the industry, until it left him behind in the shadows. Though it greeted him initially with open arms, the business never dealt him a good hand. As long as he was young, handsome and healthy, it took care of him. But when his health declined, there was nothing left for him in the land of make-believe. Without a strong and well-placed agent to fight for him, he was overlooked and neglected by the movie moguls, the men who could have taken him to the highest echelons. Perhaps with the proper breaks, he could have been another Gary Cooper or John Wayne; but those breaks never came his way.

He died far before his time. No other major B cowboy star passed away at such an age, other than by accident. Bob Steele, his partner in the Three Mesquiteers series, passed away on December 23, 1988, at the age of eight-two. He lived three decades longer than Tyler. Roy Rogers and Gene Autry lived to age 86 and 91, respectively. John Wayne bowed out at age 72, enjoying 22 more years of life than Tom was given.

Unlike many of the movie cowboys, Tyler never had a comic book issued during his lifetime. But half a century after his death, he was honored by a comic book. Published in 2003 by a group in Essex County, New York, it was a tribute to Tyler. Called "The Adirondack Cowboy, Tom Tyler Tales," it offered a biography written by Calvin Castine, a long filmography, many photos and even an original make-believe story of Tyler the cowboy.

What is the legacy of Tom Tyler? He will be long appreciated by those who enjoy film and appreciate its long and varied history. He made a lasting mark in one of the most demanding and celebrated of all professions; he was a man of substance and of style, loved by his family and friends, respected by those in his profession, and idolized by a million plus Americans at the peak of his career.

Above all, he offered a clean-cut, manly role model that may have positively impacted a portion of an entire generation of moviegoers. He had a life worth living and a life worth remembering.

Tom Tyler Filmography

(Compiled by Buck Rainey and used by permission)

1924

LEATHERSTOCKING, Pathe. 10 Chapters, George B. Seitz, director. Starring James Pierce, Edna Murphy, Harold Miller, Dave Dunbar, Frank Lackteen. Vincent Markowski, extra.

BEN HUR, MGM, 117M, Fred Niblo, director. Starring Ramon Novarro, Francis X. Bushman, Betty Bronson. Vincent Markowski, extra.

THREE WEEKS, Goldwyn, 8R. Alan Crosland, director. Staring Aileen Pringle, Conrad Nagel. Bill Burns (Vincent Markowski), extra.

LET'S GO, GALLAGHER, R-C/FBO, SR. Robert De Lacey, director. Starring Tom Tyler, Barbara Starr, Olin Francis, Frankie Darro, Alfred Hewston.

1925

THE COWBOY MUSKETEER, R-C/FBO, SR, Robert De Lacey, director. Starring Tom Tyler, Frances Dare, Frankie Darro, Jim London, David Dunbar.

THE ONLY THING, MGM, 58M. Jack Conway, director. Starring Eleanor Boardman, Conrad Nagel, Edward Connolly, Bill Burns (Vincent Markowski), extra.

THE WYOMING WILDCAT, R-C/FBO, 5R. Robert De Lacey, director. Tom Tyler, Virginia Southern, Billie Bennett, Frankie Darro, Gilbert Clayton, Ethan Laidlaw.

1926

THE ARIZONA STREAK, R-C/FBO, 5R. Robert De Lacey, director. Starring Tom Tyler, Frankie Darro, Alfred Hewston, Ada Mae Vaughn, Leroy Mason, Mary Lane, David Ward.

BORN TO BATTLE, R-C/FBO, 5R. Robert De Lacey, director. Starring Tom Tyler, Jean Arthur, Frankie Darro, Ray Childs, Fred Gambold, Leroy Mason, Ethan Laidlaw.

THE COWBOY COP, R-C/FBO, 5R. Robert De Lacey, director. Starring Tom Tyler, Jean Arthur, Frankie Darro, Arthur Irvin, Pat Harmon, Earl Haley, Beans (dog).

THE MASQUERADE BANDIT, R-C/FBO, 5R. Robert De Lacey, director. Starring Tom Tyler, Dorothy Dunbar, Frankie Darro, Ethan Laidlaw, Alfred Hewston, Ray Childs, Earl Haley.

OUT OF THE WEST, R-C/FBO, 5R. Robert De Lacey, director. Starring Tom Tyler, Bernice Welch, Frankie Darro, Harry J. O'Connor, Ethan Laidlaw, Alfred Hewston.

RED HOT HOOFS, R-C/FBO, 5R. Robert De Lacey, director. Starring Tom Tyler, Frankie Darro, Dorothy Dunbar, Harry O'Connor, Al Kaufman, Barney Furey, Stanley Taylor.

TOM AND HIS PALS, R-C/FBO, 5R. Robert De Lacey, director. Starring Tom Tyler, Doris Hill, Frankie Darro, Helen Lynch, Leroy Mason, Dickie Brandon, Frank Woods, Beans.

WILD TO GO, R-C/FBO, 5R. Robert De Lacey, director. Starring Tom Tyler, Eugenia Gilbert, Frankie Darro, Fred Burns, Ethan Laidlaw, Earl Haley.

1927

THE CHEROKEE KID, R-C/FBO, 5R. Robert De Lacey, director. Starring Tom Tyler, Sharon Lynn, Jerry Pembroke, Robert Burns, Bob Reeves, Carol Holloway, Frankie Darro.

CYCLONE OF THE RANGE, R-C/FBO, 5R. Robert De Lacey, director. Starring Tom Tyler, Elsie Tarron, Harry O'Connor, Frankie Darro, Richard Howard, Harry Woods.

THE DESERT PIRATE, FBO, 5R. James Dugan, director. Starring Tom Tyler, Frankie Darro, Duane Thompson, Edward Hearn, Tom Lingham, Vester Pegg, Alfred Hewston.

THE FLYING U. RANCH, R-C/FBO, 5R. Robert De Lacey, director. Starring Tom Tyler, Nora Lane, Frankie Darro, Bert Hadley, Grace Woods, Barney Furey, Bill Patton.

LIGHTNING LARIATS, R-C/FBO, 5R. Robert De Lacey, director. Starring Tom Tyler, Dorothy Dunbar, Frankie Darro, Ruby Blaine, Fred Holmes, Irvin Renard, Carl Silvers.

THE SONORA KID, R-C/FBO, 5R. Robert De Lacey, director. Starring Tom Tyler, Peggy Montgomery, Billie Bennett, Mark Hamilton, Jack Richardson, Ethan Laidlaw, Bruce Gordon.

SPLITTING THE BREEZE, R-C/FBO, 5R. Robert De Lacey, director. Starring Tom Tyler, Peggy Montgomery, Harry Woods, Barney Furey, Tom Lingham, Alfred Hewston.

TOM'S GANG, R-C/FBO, 5R. Robert De Lacey, director. Starring Tom Tyler, Sharon Lynn, Frankie Darro, Harry Woods, Frank Rice, Barney Furey, Tom Lingham.

1928

THE AVENGING RIDER, FBO, 5R. Wallace Fox, director. Starring Tom Tyler, Frankie Darro, Florence Allen, Al Ferguson, Bob Fleming, Arthur Thalasso, Mal Davis.

PHANTOM OF THE RANGE, FBO, 5R. James Dugan, director. Starring Tom Tyler, Duane Thompson, Frankie Darro, Charles McHugh, James Pierce, Marjorie Zier.

TERROR MOUNTAIN, FBO, 5R. Louis King, director. Starring Tom Tyler, Ione Reed, Frankie Darro, Al Ferguson, Jules Cowles.

THE TEXAS TORNADO, FBO, 5R. Frank Hwoard Clark, director. Starring Tom Tyler, Nora Lane, Frankie Darro, Bob Burns, Jack Anthony, Frank Whitson.

TYRANT OF RED GULCH, FBO, 5R. Robert De Lacey, director. Starring Tom Tyler, Frankie Darro, Josephine Borio, Harry Woods, Barney Furey, Serge Temoff.

WHEN THE LAW RIDES, FBO, 5R. Robert De Lacey, director. Starring Tom Tyler, Ione Reed, Frankie Darro, Harry O'Connor, Harry Woods, Barney Furey, Charles Thurston.

1929

GUN LAW, FBO, 5R. Robert De Lacey, director. Starring Tom Tyler, Ethlyne Clair, Frankie Darro, Harry Woods, Lew Meehan, Tom Brooker.

IDAHO RED, FBO, 5R. Robert De Lacey, director. Starring Tom Tyler, Frankie Darro, Patricia Caron, Barney Furey, Lew Meehan, Yakima Canutt, Albert J. Smith.

LAW OF THE PLAINS, Syndicate, 5R. J.P. McGowan, director. Starring Tom Tyler, Natalie Joyce, Al Ferguson, J.P. McGowan, William Nolte, Francis Walker.

THE LONE HORSEMAN, Syndicate, 5R. J.P. McGowan, director. Starring Tom Tyler, Charlotte Winn, J.P. McGowan, Blackjack Ward, Tom Bay, Mack V. Wright.

THE MAN FROM NEVADA, Syndicate, 5R. J.P. McGowan, director. Starring Tom Tyler, Natalie Joyce, Al Ferguson, Alfred Hewston, Kip Cooper, Godfrey Craig, Cliff Lyons.

'NEATH WESTERN SKIES, Syndicate, 5R. J.P. McGowan, director. Starring Tom Tyler, Lotus Thompson, Hank Bell, Harry Woods, J. P. McGowan, Bobby Dunn, Barney Furey.

THE PHANTOM RIDER, Syndicate, 5R. J. P. McGowan, director. Starring Tom Tyler, Lotus Thompson, Harry Woods, J.P. MCGowan.

PIONEERS OF THE WEST, Syndicate, 5R. J. P. McGowan, director. Starring Tom Tyler, Charlotte Winn, J. P. McGowan, George Brownhill, Mack V. Wright, Tom Bay.

THE PRIDE OF THE PAWNEE, FBO/RKO, 5R. Robert De Lacey, director. Starring Tom Tyler, Ethlyne Clair, Frankie Darro, Barney Furey, Lew Meehan, Jack Hilliard.

TRAIL OF THE HORSE THIEVES, FBO, 5R. Robert De Lacey, director. Starring Tom Tyler, Sharon Lynn, Frankie Darro, Harry O'Connor, Barney Furey, Bill Nestell, Vic Allen.

1930

CALL OF THE DESERT, Syndicate, 5R. J. P. McGowan, director. Starring Tom Tyler, Sheila LeGay, Bud Osborne, Cliff Lyons, Bobby Dunn.

THE CANYON OF MISSING MEN, Syndicate, 5R. J. P. McGowan, director. Starring Tom Tyler, Sheila LeGay, Tom Forman, Bud Osborne, J. P. McGowan, Cliff Lyons, Bobby Dunn.

HALF-PINT MOLLY, Pathe, 2R. Starring Tom Tyler, Mona Ray, Bud Osborne, Harry O'Connor, Hank McFarlene, Marcio Manning, Al Smith, Bobby Dunn.

THE PHANTOM OF THE WEST, Mascot, 10 chapters. Ross Lederman, director. Starring Tom Tyler, William Desmond, Dorothy Gulliver, Joe Bonomo, Tom Santschi.

1931

BATTLING WITH BUFFALO BILL, Universal, 12 chapters. Ray Taylor, director. Starring Tom Tyler, Rex Bell, Lucille Brown, William Desmond, Francis Ford, Yakima Canutt, Jim Thorpe.

GALLOPING THRU, Monogram, 58M. Lloyd Nosler, director. Starring Tom Tyler, Betty Mack, Al Bridge, Si Jenks, Stanley Blystonbe, G. D. Wood.

GOD'S COUNTRY AND THE MAN, Syndicate, 59M. J. P. McGowan, director. Staring Tom Tyler, Betty Mack, George Hayes, Ted Adams, Julian Rivero, Al Bridge, John Elliott.

THE MAN FROM DEATH VALLEY, Monogram, 64M. Lloyd Nosler, director. Staring Tom Tyler, Betty Mack, John Oscar, Si Jenks, Gino Corrado, Stanley Blystone.

PARTNERS OF THE TRAIL, Monogram, 63M. Wallace Fox, director. Starring Tom Tyler, Betty Mack, Lafe McKee, Horace B. Carpenter, Hank Bell, Reginald Sheffield, Pat Rooney.

A RIDER OF THE PLAINS, Syndicate, 57M. J. P. McGowan, director. Starring Tom Tyler, Andy Shuford, Lilian Bond, Al Bridge, Ted Adams, Gordon DeMain, Jack Perrin.

TWO-FISTED JUSTICE, Monogram, 63M. G. Arthur Durlam, director. Starring Tom Tyler, Barbara Weeks, Bobby Nelson, Yakima Canutt, John Elliott, G.D. Wood.

WEST OF CHEYENNE, Syndicate, 56M. Harry S. Webb, director. Starring Tom Tyler, Josephine Hill, Harry Woods, Robert Walker, Ben Corbett, Fern Emmett, Lafe McKee, Lew Meehan.

1932

THE FORTY-NINERS, Freuler/Monarch. 59M. John P. McCarthy, director. Starring Tom Tyler, Betty Mack, Al Bridge, Fern Emmett, G.D. Wood.

HONOR OF THE MOUNTED, Monogram, 62M. Harry Fraser, director. Starring Tom Tyler, Cecilia Ryland, Francis McDonald, Charles King, Tom London, Stanley Blystone.

JUNGLE MYSTERY, Universal, 12 chapters. Ray Taylor, director. Starring Tom Tyler, Cecilia Parker, William Desmond, Philo McCullough, Noah Beery Jr., Sam Baker.

THE MAN FROM NEW MEXICO, Monogram, 60M. J.P. McCarthy, director, Starring Tom Tyler, Caryl Lincoln, Robert Walker, Jack Richardson, Lafe McKeee, Frank Ball, Slim Whitaker.

SINGLE-HANDED SANDERS, Monogram, 61M.. Lloyd Nosler, director. Starring Tom Tyler, Margaret Morris, Robert Manning, G.D. Wood, John Elliott, Hank Bell, Lois Bridge.

VANISHING MEN, Monogram, 62 M. Harry Fraser, director. Starring Tom Tyler, Adele Lacy, John Elliott, Raymond Keane, William A. Thorne, Charles King, Robert Manning.

1933

CLANCY OF THE MOUNTED, Universal, 12 chapters. Ray Taylor, director. Starring Tom Tyler, Jacqueline Wells (Julie Bishop), William Desmond, Rosalie Roy, Francis Ford, Tom London.

DEADWOOD PASS, Freuler/Monarch, 62M. J. P. McGowan, director. Starring Tom Tyler, Alice Dahl, Wally Wales, Buffalo Bill Jr., Lafe McKee, Bud Osborne, Edmund Cobb.

THE PHANTOM OF THE AIR, Universal, 12 chapters. Ray Taylor, director. Starring Tom Tyler, Gloria Shea, LeRoy Mason, Hugh Enfield, William Desmond, Walter Brennan.

WAR OF THE RANGE, Freuler/Monarch, 59M. J.P. McGowan, director. Starring Tom Tyler, Caryl Lincoln, Lane Chandler, Lafe McKee, Slim Witkaer, Charles K. French.

WHEN A MAN RIDES ALONE, Freuler/Monarch, 60M. J.P. McGowan, director. Starring Tom Tyler, Adele Lacy, Alan Bridge, Robert Burns, Frank Ball, Jack Rockwell, Alma Chester.

1934

RIDIN' THRU, Reliable/Steiner, 55M. Harry S. Webb, director. Starring Tom Tyler, Lafe McGee, Philo McCullough, Ben Corbett, Lew Meehan, Bud Osborne, Ruth Hiatt.

1935

BORN TO BATTLE, Reliable/Steiner, 63M, Harry S Webb, director. Starring Tom Tyler, Jean Carmen, Earl Dwire, Julian Rivero, William Desmond, Charles King.

COYOTE TRAILS, Reliable/Steiner. 65M. B. B. Ray, director. Starring Tom Tyler, Helen Dahl, Ben Corbett, Lafe McKee, Dick Alexander, Roger Williams, George Chesebro.

THE FIGHTING HERO, Reliable/Steiner. 55M. Harry S. Webb, director. Starring Tom Tyler, Renee Borden, Edward Hearn, Dick Botiller, Ralph Lewis, Murdock McQuerrie.

THE LARAMIE KID, Reliable/Steiner. 57M, Harry S. Webb, director. Starring Tom Tyler, Alberta Vaughn, Al Ferguson, Murdock McQuerrie, George Chesebro.

MYSTERY RANCH, Reliable/Steiner, 56M. Ray Bernard (Bernard B. Ray) director. Starring Tom Tyler, Roberta Gale, Jack Gable (Jack Perrin), Charles King.

POWDERSMOKE RANGE, RKO, 71M. Wallace Fox, director. Starring Harry Carey, Hoot Gibson, Tom Tyler, Guinn "Big Boy" Williams, Bob Steele, Wally Wales, Art Mix.

RIO RATTLER, Reliable/Steiner. 58M. Franklin Shamray (B. B. Ray), director. Starring Tom Tyler, Marion Shilling, Eddie Gribbon, William Gould, Tom London, Lafe McKee.

SILENT VALLEY, Reliable/Steiner. 56M. B. B. Ray, director. Starring Tom Tyler, Nancy DeShon, Wally Wales, Charles King, Alan Bridge, George Chesebro.

THE SILVER BULLET, Reliable/Steiner. 59M. B. B. Ray, director. Starring Tom Tyler, Jayne Regan, Lafe McKee, Charles King, Slim Whitaker, Franklyn Farnum, Hank Bell.

TERROR OF THE PLAINS, Reliable/Steiner. 58M, Harry S. Webb, director. Starring Tom Tyler, Roberta Gale, William Gould, Slim Whitaker, Fern Emmett, Nelson McDowell.

TRACY RIDES, Reliable/Steiner, 51M. Harry S. Webb, director. Starring Tom Tyler, Virginia Brown Faire, Edmund Cobb, Charles K. French, Lafe McKee, George Chesebro.

THE UNCONQUERED BANDIT, Reliable/Steiner. 57M. Harry W. Webb director. Starring Tom Tyler, Lillian Gilmore, Slim Whitaker, William Gould, John Elliott.

1936

FAST BULLETS, Reliable/Steiner. 57M. Henri Samuels (Harry S. Webb) director. Starring Tom Tyler, Rex Lease, Margaret Nearing, Al Bridge, William Gould.

THE LAST OUTLAW, RKO. 63M. Christy Cabanne, director. Starring Harry Carey, Hoot Gibson, Tom Tyler, Henry B. Wathall, Margaret Callahan, Ray Meyer. Fred Scott.

THE PHANTOM OF THE RANGE, Victory. 57M. Bob Hill, director. Starring Tom Tyler, Beth Marion, Sammy Cohen, Soledad Jiminez, Forest Taylor, Charles King.

PINTO RUSTLERS, Reliable/Steiner, 56M. Henri Samuels (Harry S. Webb) director. Starring Tom Tyler, Catherine Cotter, Earl Dwire, George Walsh, Al St. John.

RIDIN' ON, Reliable/Steiner. 56M. B. B. Ray, director. Starring Tom Tyler, Geraine Geear (Joan Barclay), Rex Lease, John Elliott, Earl Dwire, Wally West.

RIP ROARIN' BUCKAROO, Victory. 58M. Robert Hill director. Starring Tom Tyler, Beth Marion, Sammy Cohen, Charles King, Forrest Taylor, Richard Cramer.

ROAMIN' WILD, Reliable/Steiner. 58M. B. B. Ray, director. Starring Tom Tyler, Carol Wyndham, Max Davidson, Al Ferguson, George Chesebro, Fred Parker.

SANTA FE BOUND, Reliable/Steiner. 56M. Henri Samuels (Harry S. Webb.), director. Starring Tom Tyler, Jeanne Martel, Richard Cramer, Charles (Slim) Whitaker.

TRIGGER TOM, Reliable/Steiner. 57M. Henri Samuels, director. Starring Tom Tyler, Al St. John, Bernadene Hayes, William Gould, John Elliott, Wally Wales.

1937

BROTHERS OF THE WEST, Victory. 58M. Sam Katzman, director. Starring Tom Tyler, Lois Wilde, Dorothy Short, Lafe McKee, Bob Terry, Roger Williams, Jim Corey.

CHEYENNE RIDES AGAIN, Victory. 56M. Bob Hill, director. Starring Tom Tyler, Lucile Browne Creighton (Lon Jr.) Chaney, Roger Williams, Carmen LaRoux.

THE FEUD OF THE TRAIL, Victory. 56M. Bob Hill, director. Starring Tom Tyler, Harlene Wood, Milburn Morante, Lafe McKee, Roger Williams, Jim Corey.

LOST RANCH, Victory. 56M. Sam Katzman, director. Starring Tom Tyler, Jeanne Martel, Marjorie Beebe, Howard Bryant, Ted Lorch, Slim Whitaker, Forrest Taylor.

MYSTERY RANGE, Victory. 56M. Bob Hill, director. Starring Tom Tyler, Jerry Bergh, Milburn Morante, Lafe McKee, Roger Williams, Dick Alexander, Jim Corey.

ORPHAN OF THE PECOS, Victory. 55M. Sam Katzman, director. Starring Tom Tyler, Jeanne Martel, Lafe McKee, Forrest Taylor, Ted Lorch, Slim Whitaker, John Elliott.

1938

KING OF ALCATRAZ, Paramount 56M. Robert Florey, director. Staring Gail Patrick, Lloyd Nolan, J. Carrol Naish, Anthony Quinn, Dennis Morgan, Tom Tyler, Harry Carey.

1939

DRUMS ALONG THE MOHAWK, TCF. 103M. John Ford, director. Starring Henry Fonda, Claudette Colbert, Edna May Oliver, Ward Bond, John Carradine, Eddie Collins, Tom Tyler.

FRONTIER MARSHAL, TCF. 71M. Allan Dwan, director. Starring Randolph Scott, Nancy Kelly, Cesar Romero, Binnie Barnes, John Carradine, Ward Bond, Tom Tyler.

GONE WITH THE WIND, Selznick/MGM. 225M. Victory Fleming, Sam Wood, George Cukor, directors. Starring Vivien Leigh, Clark Gable, Olivia de Havilland, Leslie Howard, Thomas Mitchell, Hattie McDaniel, Tom Tyler, Yakima Canutt.

THE NIGHT RIDERS, Republic. 58M. George Sherman, director. Starring John Wayne, Ray Corrigan, Max Terhune, Ruth Rogers, Doreen McKay, Tom Tyler, George Douglas.

STAGECOACH, United Artists. 96M. John Ford, director. Starring John Wayne, Claire Trevor, Thomas Mitchell, John Carradine, Andy Devine, George Bancroft, Tim Holt, Tom Tyler.

1940

BROTHER ORCHID, Warner Brothers. 91M. Lloyd Bacon, director. Starring Edward G. Robinson, Ann Sothern, Humphrey Bogart, Ralph Bellamy, Donald Crisp, Tom Tyler.

CHEROKEE STRIP, Paramount. 86M. Lesley Selander, director. Starring Richard Dix, Florence Rice, William Henry, Victor Jory, Andy Clyde, Tom Tyler, George E. Stone.

THE GRAPES OF WRATH, TCF. 129M. John Ford, director. Starring Henry Fonda, Jane Darwell, John Carradine, Charley Grapewin. Doris Bowden, Russell Simpson, Tom Tyler.

THE LIGHT OF WESTERN STARS, Paramount. 67M. Lesley Selander, director. Starring Russell Hayden, Victor Jory, Jo Ann Sayers, Noah Beery, Jr., Tom Tyler.

THE MUMMY'S HAND, Universal. 67M. Christy Cabanne, director. Starring Dick Foran, Peggy Moran, Eduardo Cianelli, Wallace Ford, George Zucco, Tom Tyler.

TEXAS RANGERS RIDE AGAIN, Paramount. 68M. James Hogan, director. Starring John Howard, Ellen Drew, Akim Tamiroff, Broderick Crawford, Tom Tyler, Charley Grapewin.

THE WESTERNER, United Artist. 100M. William Wyler, director. Starring Gary Cooper, Walter Brennan, Fred Stone, Diris Davenport, Dana Andrews, Forrest Tucker, Tom Tyler.

1941

ADVENTURES OF CAPTAIN MARVEL, Republic. 12 Chapters. William Witney, John English, directors. Starring Tom Tyler, Frank Coghlan, Jr., William Benedict, Louise Currie, Robert Strange.

BAD MEN OF MISSOURI, Warner Brothers. 72M. Ray Enright, director. Starring Dennis Morgan, Jany Wyman, Wayne Morris, Arthur Kennedy, Tom Tyler.

BORDER VIGILANTES, Paramount. 62M. Derwin Abrahams, director. Starring William Boyd, Andy Clyde, Russell Hayden, Victor Jory, Morris Ankrum, Tom Tyler, Hal Taliaferro.

BUCK PRIVATES, Universal. 82M. Arthur Libin, director. Starring Bud Abbott, Lou Costello, Andrews Sister, Nat Pendleton, Lee Bowman, Alan Curtis, Jane Frazee, Tom Tyler.

GAUCHOS OF EL DORADO, Republic. 56M. Les Orlebeck, director. Starring Bob Steele, Tom Tyler, Rufe Davis, Lois Collier, Duncan Renaldo, Yakima Canutt, Eddie Dean.

RIDERS OF THE TIMBERLINE, Paramount. 59M. Lesley Selander, director. Starring William Boyd, Andy Clyde, Brad King, J. Farrell MacDonald, Eleanor Stewart, Tom Tyler.

WEST OF CIMARRON, Republic. 56M. Les Orlebeck, director. Starring Bob Steele, Tom Tyler, Rufe Davis, Lois Collier, James Bush, Guy Usher, Hugh Prosser, Roy Barcroft.

1942

CODE OF THE OUTLAW, Republic. 57M. John English, director. Starring Bob Steele, Tom Tyler, Rufe Davis, Melinda Leighton, Weldon Heyburn, Don Curtis, John Ince.

THE MUMMY'S TOMB, Universal. 61M. Harold Young, director. Starring Lon Chaney, Jr., Dick Foran, John Hubbard, Elyse Knox, George Zucco, Wallace Ford, Tom Tyler, Turhan Bey.

THE PHANTOM PLAINSMEN, Republic. 65M. John English, director. Starring Bob Steele, Tom Tyler, Rufe Davis, Lois Collier, Robert O. Davis, Charles Miller, Alex Callam.

RAIDERS OF THE RANGE, Republic. 55M. John English, director. Starring Bob Steele, Tom Tyler, Rufe Davis, Lois Collier, Fred Kohler, Jr., Dennis Moore, Frank Jacquet.

SHADOWS ON THE SAGE, Republic. 58M. Les Orlebeck, director. Starring Bob Steele, Tom Tyler, Jimmie Dodd, Cheryl Walker, Harry Holman, Yakima Canutt, Tom London.

THE TALK OF THE TOWN, Columbia. 118M. George Stevens, director. Starring Cary Grant, Jean Arthur, Ronald Colman, Edgar Buchanan, Glenda Farrell, Tom Tyler, Rex Ingram.

VALLEY OF HUNTED MEN, Republic. 60M. John English, director. Starring Bob Steele, Tom Tyler, Jimmie Dodd, Anna Marie Steward, Edward Van Sloan, Roland Varno.

VALLEY OF THE SUN, RKO. 79M. George Marshall, director. Starring James Craig, Lucille Ball, Dean Jagger, Billy Gilbert, Cedric Hardwicke, Tom Tyler, Antonio Moreno.

WESTWARD HO, Republic. 56M. John English, director. Starring Bob Steele, Tom Tyler, Rufe Davis, Evelyn Brent, Donald Curtis, Lois Collier, Emmett Lynn, John James, Milton Kibbee.

1943

THE BLOCKED TRAIL, Republic. 58M. Elmer Clifton, director. Starring Bob Steele, Tom Tyler, Jimmie Dodd, Helen Deverell, George J. Lewis, Charles Miller, Kermit Maynard.

THE PHANTOM, Columbia. 15 Chapters. B. Reeves Eason, director. Starring Tom Tyler, Jeanne Bates, Kenneth MacDonald, Frank Shannon, Guy Kingsford, Ernie Adams, Age (dog).

RIDERS OF THE RIO GRANDE, Republic. 55M. Howard Bretherton, director. Starring Bob Steele, Tom Tyler, Jimmie Dodd, Lorraine Miller, Edward Van Sloan, Rick Vallin.

SANTA FE SCOUTS, Republic. 57M. Howard Bretherton, director. Starring Bob Steele, Tom Tyler, Jimmie Dodd, Lois Collier, John James, Tom Chatterton, Tom London, Jack Ingram.

THUNDERING TRAILS, Republic. 56M. John English, director. Starring Bob Steele, Tom Tyler, Jimmie Dodd, Nell O'Day, Sam Flint, Charles Miller, Karl Hackett.

WAGON TRACKS WEST, Republic. 55M. Starring Bill Elliott, George Hayes, Tom Tyler, Anne Jeffreys, Robert Frazer, Rick Vallin, Roy Barcroft, Tom London.

1944

BOSS OF BOOMTOWN, Universal. 58M. Ray Taylor, director. Starring Rod Cameron, Fuzzy Knight, Tom Tyler, Vivian Austin (Coe), Ray Whitley, Jack Ingram, Robert Barron.

GUN TO GUN, Warner Brothers. 20M. D. Ross Lederman, director. Starring Robert Shayne, Lupita Tovar, Pedro De Cordova, Harry Woods, Tom Tyler, Anita Camargo, Julian Rivero.

LADIES OF WASHINGTON, TCF. Louis King, director. Starring Trudy Marshall, Ronald Graham, Anthony Quinn, Sheila Ryan, Robert Bailey, Jackie Paley, Tom Tyler.

THE NAVY WAY, Paramount. 6R. William Berke, director. String Robert Lowery, Jean Parker, William Henry, Roscoe Karns, Sheron Douglas, Richard Powers, Tom Tyler.

1945

SAN ANTONIO, Warner Brothers. 111M. David Butler, director. Starring Errol Flynn, Alexis Smith. S. Z. Sakall, Florence Bates, John Litel, Paul Kelly, Tom Tyler, Monte Blue.

SING ME A SONG OF TEXAS, Columbia. 66M. Vernon Keays, director. Starring Tom Tyler, Rosemary Lane, Hoosier Hotshots, Hal McIntyre and his Orchestra, Guinn Williams.

THEY WERE EXPENDABLE, MGM. 135M. John Ford, director. Starring Robert Montgomery, John Wayne, Donna Reed, Jack Holt, Ward Bond, Marshall Thompson, Tom Tyler.

1946

BADMAN'S TERRITORY, RKO. 98M. Tim Whelan, director. Starring Randolph Scott, Ann Richards, George Hayes, Lawrence Tierney, Tom Tyler, John Halloran, Steve Brodie.

NEVER SAY GOODBYE, Warner Brothers. 97M. James V. Kern, director. Starring Errol Flynn, Eleanor Parker. S. Z. Sakall, Hattie McDaniel, Lucile Watson, Forrest Tucker, Tom Tyler.

1947

CHEYENNE, Warner Brothers. 100M. Raoul Walsh, director. Starring Dennis Morgan, Jane Wyman, Arthur Kennedy, Janis Paige, Bruce Bennett, Barton MacLane, Bob Steele, Tom Tyler.

1948

BLOOD ON THE MOON, RKO. 88M. Robert Wise, director. Starring Robert Mitchum, Barbara Bel Geddes, Robert Preston, Walter Brennan, Phyllis Thaxter, Tom Tyler.

THE DUDE GOES WEST, American Artist. 86M. Kurt Neumann, director. Starring Eddie Albert, Gale Storm, James Gleason, Gilbert Roland, Barton MacLane, Tom Tyler, Binnie Barnes.

THE GOLDEN EYE, Monogram. 69M. William Beaudine, director. Starring Roland Winters, Manton Moreland, Victor Sen Yung, Wanda McKay, Tim Ryan, Edmund Cobb, Tom Tyler.

RED RIVER, United Artists. 125M. Howard Hawks, director. Starring John Wayne, Joanne Dru, Montgomery Clift, Walter Brennan, Coleen Gray, Harry Carey, Tom Tyler, Noah Beery, Jr.

RETURN OF THE BAD MEN, RKO. 96M. Ray Enright, director. Starring Randolph Scott, Robert Ryan, Anne Jeffreys, George Hayes, Jacqueline White, Tom Tyler, Richard Powers.

THE THREE MUSKETEERS, MGM. 125M. George Sydney, director. Starring Lana Turner, Gene Kelly, June Allyson, Van Heflin, Angela Lansbury, Frank Morgan, Tom Tyler.

1949

I SHOT JESSE JAMES, Lippert. 81M. Samuel Fuller, director. Starring John Ireland, Preston Foster, Barbara Britton, J. Edward Bromberg, Victor Killian, Tom Tyler.

SAMSON AND DELILAH, Paramount. 131M. Robert Florey, director. Starring Victor Mature, Hedy Lamarr, George Sanders, Angela Lansbury, Henry Wilcoxin, Fay Holden, Tom Tyler.

THE YOUNGER BROTHERS, Warner Brothers. 77M. Edwin L. Marin, director. Starring Wayne Morris, Janis Paige, Bruce Bennett, Geraldine Brooks, Robert Hutton, Tom Tyler, Monte Blue.

1950

OUTLAWS OF TEXAS, Monogram. 56M. Thomas Carr, director. Starring Whip Wilson, Andy Clyde, Phyllis Coates, Terry Frost, Tom Tyler.

TRAIL OF ROBIN HOOD, Republic. 66M. William Witney, director. Starring Roy Rogers, Penny Edwards, Gordon Jones, Jack Holt, with guest appearances by Rex Allen, Monte Hale, Rocky Lane, Tom Tyler and Crash Corrigan.

1951

KING OF THE BULLWHIP, Western Adventure. 59M. Starring Lash LaRue, Al St. John, Jack Holt, Tom Neal, Anne Gwynne, Tom Tyler.

1952

OUTLAW WOMEN, Howco. 73M. Sam Newfield, director. Starring Marie Windsor, Richard Rober, Allan Nixon, Jackie Coogan, Maria Hart, Tom Tyler, Carla Balenda.

ROAD AGENT, RLP. 60M. Lesley Selander, director. Starring Tim Holt, Richard Martin, Noreen Nash, Mauritz Hugo, Tom Tyler, Edward Hearn, Stanley Blystone.

THE YELLOW HAIRED KID, Monogram. 72M. Frank McDonald, director. Starring Gary Madison, Andy Devine, Alan Hale, Jr., Marcia Mae Jones, Riley Hill, David Bruce, Tom Tyler.

1953

COW COUNTRY, Allied Artists, 93M. Lesley Seladner, director. Starring Edmond O'Brien, Raymond Hatton, Robert Lowery, Peggie Castle, Tom Tyler, Lance Chandler.

TV PILOT: THE ADVENTURES OF THE TUCSON KID, Tucson Kid Productions. 30M. Starring Tom Keene, Tom Tyler, Lyle Talbot, Keene Duncan, Harvey B. Dunn, Edward D. Wood, Jr.

Bibliography

1. *Hollywood: 1920-1970,* by David Robinson, A.S. Barnes and Company, 1997.
2. *A Flame of Pure Fire: Jack Dempsey and The Roaring '20s,* by Roger Kahn, Harcourt Brace & Company, 1999.
3. i.e. an Autobiography, by Mickey Rooney, G. P. Putnam's Sons, 1965.
4. *Ladies of the Western,* by Michael G. Fitzgerald and Boyd Magers, McFarland, 2002.
5. *Shazam: From the '40s to the '70s,* by E. Nelson Birdwell, Harmony Books, 1977.
6. *Tarzan of the Movies,* by Gabe Essoe, The Citadel Press, 1968,
7. *The Edge,* by Howard E. Ferguson, TheEdge Company, 1990.
8. *Those Fabulous Movie Years: The 30s,* by Albert R. Leventhal, Barre Publishing, 1975.
9. *The Strongman: The Daredevil Exploits of the Mightiest Man in the Movies,* by Joe Bonomo, published by Bonomo Studios, Inc, 1958.
10. *Where's The Rest of Me,* by Ronald Reagan, Duell, Sloan and Pearce, 1965
11. *Hollywood Corral,* by Don Miller, Popular Library, 1975.
12. *The Thrill of It All,* by Alan G. Barbour, Collier Books, 1971.
13. *Days of Thrills and Adventures,* by Alan G. Barbour, Collier Books, 1970.
14. *The Westerns: From Silents to Cinerama,* by George N. Fenin and William K. Everson, The Orion Press, 1962.
15. *A Pictorial History of the Western Film,* by William K. Everson, The Citadel Press, 1975, page 96
16. *Sound Films 1927-1929, A United States Filmography* by Alan G. Fetrow, Tyler is listed in "During the Evacuation" sequence as "commanding officer."
17. *Trail Talk,* by Bobby J. Copeland, Empire Publishing, Inc, 1996.
18. *The Iron Game,* by David Webster, Irvine, 1976.

Footnotes:

1. *The Westerns: From Silents to Cinerama,* by George N. Fenin and William K. Everson, The Orion Press, 1962, page 99.
2. Ibid, pages 114, 115.
3. *Where's The Rest of Me,* by Ronald Reagan, Duell, Sloan and Pearce, 1965, page 17.
4. Email letter from Tom Karkowski, 2003.
5. *Hollywood: 1920-1970,* by David Robinson, A.S. Barnes and Company, 1997, page 13.

6. *A Flame of Pure Fire: Jack Dempsey and The Roaring '20s,* by Roger Kahn, Harcourt Brace & Company, 1999, page 112.
7. *Hollywood: 1920-1970,* by David Robinson, page 20.
8. *Hollywood: 1920-1970,* by David Robinson, page 21.
9. The Old Corral web site, Chuck Anderson.
10. By Bobby Copeland, page 18.
11. *Hollywood: 1920-1970,* by David Robinson, page 17.
12. *The Westerns: From Silents to Cinerama,* by George N. Fenin and William K. Everson, The Orion Press, 1962, page 117
13. *Old West* magazine, issue Winter 1974, article by Glenn Shirley.
14. The Life and Legend of Tom Mix, by Paul E. Mix, A.S. Barnes & Company, 1972, page 114.
15. *The Iron Game,* by David Webster, Irvine, 1976, page 115.
16. Interview with Bruce Bennett, Los Angeles, 1999.
17. Calvin Castine email.
18. *The Strongman: The Daredevil Exploits of the Mightiest Man in the Movies,* by Joe Bonomo, published by Bonomo Studios, Inc, 1958, page 280.
19. *Old West* magazine, issue Winter 1974, by Glenn Shirley.
20. *The Thrill of It All,* by Alan Barbour, Collier Books, 1971, page 13.
21. *Those Fabulous Movie Years: The 30s,* by Albert R. Leventhal, page 5.
22. *Hollywood: 1920-1970,* by David Robinson, page 64.
23. *Old West* magazine, issue Winter 1974, by Glenn Shirley.
24. *Written, Produced and Directed by Oliver Drake,* by Oliver Drake.
25. *The Edge,* by Howard E. Ferguson, The Edge Company, 1990, page 2-18.
26. *Hollywood Corral, by Don Miller,* Popular Library, 1974, page 50.
27. *Those Fabulous Movie Years: The 30s,* by Albert R. Leventhal , page 9.
28. Ibid, page 9.
29. *Western Women,* by Boyd Magers and Michael G. Fitzgerald, 1999, page 197.
30. *Hollywood Corral,* by Don Miller, page 49.
31. *Hollywood Corral,* by Don Miller, Popular Library, 1974, page 48.
32. *Trail Talk,* by Bobby Copeland, Empire Publishing, 1997, page 143.
33. *Wrangler's Roost,* article in No 118. by Bruce Hickey.
34. *Winners of the West,* Karlton LaRue.
35. *Tom Tyler and George O'Brien: The Herculeses of the Cinema Range,* by Mario DeMarco, page 6.
36. Jean Carmen, in conversation with Bobby Copeland at a Charlotte Film Festival.
37. *Trail Talk,* by Bobby Copeland, Empire Publishing, 1996, page 118.
38. *Old West* magazine, issue Winter 1974, by Glenn Shirley, page 14.
39. *Shooting Star,* by Maurice Zolotow.
40. *Hollywood Corral,* by Don Miller, page 51.
41. *Sound Films 1927-1929, A United States Filmography* by Alan G. Fetrow, Tyler is listed in "During the Evacuation" sequence as "commanding officer."
42. *Days of Thrills and Adventure,* by Alan Barbour, Collier Books, 1970, page 59.
43. Ibid, page 27.
44. Quotes from Witney: *In a Door, Into a Fight Out a Door, Into a Chase,* page 59.

45. Quotes by Frank Coughlin From an interview by Gregory Jackson, Jr. in *"Serial World."*
46. Quotes by Billy Benedict quote from a "Cliffhanger" interview by Joe Collura.
47. Quotes by Coughlin , From an interview by Gregory Jackson, Jr. in *"Serial World."*
48. *The Great Movie Serials,* by Jim Harmon and Donald F. Glut, Doubleday & Company 1972, page 219.
49. Ibid, page 222.
50. *Famous Monsters of Filmland,* issue No. 101, September 1973, page 21.
51. Ibid, page 223.
52. *Big Reel,* issue #262, March 1966, "Tom Tyler, Super Hero," article by William C. Cline, page 108.
53. Quotes by Coughlin.
54. *Cliffhanger,* issue # 10, 1988, article by Joseph Collura, page 62.
55. *Ladies of the Western,* by Michael G. Fitzgerald and Boyd Magers, McFarland, 2002, page 38.
56. Email letter from Patty Forecast, assistant for Louise C. Good, received July 21, 2003
57. *Shazam: From the '40s to the '70s,* by E. Nelson Birdwell, Harmony Books, 1977, page 14-15.
58. *FCA #55,* published by P.C. Hamerlinck, Spring 1996.
59. *Hollywood Studio Magazine,* Volume 14, No. 10, author not listed, page 12.
60. *Tarzan of the Movies,* by Gabe Essoe, The Citadel Press, 1968, page 67.
61. *"A Visit with Lee Falk,"* by A. Tollin, Comics Revue, Vol.1 No.27, 1988.
62. *"The Great Movie Serials,"* by Jim Harmon and Donald F. Glut, page 268.
63. *Big Reel,* issue #262, March 1966, "Tom Tyler, Super Hero," article by William C. Cline, page 108.
64. *"The Great Movie Serials,"* by Jim Harmon and Donald F. Glut
65. *Those Fabulous Movie Years: The 30s,* by Albert R. Leventhal, page 11.
66. *The Encyclopedia of Westerns,* by Herb Fagen, Checkmark Books, 2003, pages 388-89.
67. Author interview with Jean Hale, wife of Monte Hale.
68. *Hollywood Corral,* by Don Miller, page 48.
69. i.e. an Autobiography, by Mickey Rooney, G. P. Putnam's Sons, 1965, page 237.
70. Western Clippings magazine, *#16, March/April 1997,* "Cowboy Quotes."
71. *Hollywood Corral,* by Don Miller, page 51.
72. *Under Western Skies,* by Stormy Weathers.
73. The Old Corral web site, Chuck Anderson.

Interviews by the Author

June, 1998, in Los Angeles, with Bruce Bennett (aka Herman Brix), at his home.
January 28, 2004, phone interview with Marilyn Beaudrie, on January 28, 2004.
August 14, 2004, in Detroit, with Ray and Joanne Slepski, Marilyn Beaudrie, Tom and Betty Kozyra, and Tony and Susie Redge.
October 15, 2004, phone interview with Sandy Slepski.
October 15, 2004, in Victorville, California, with Mike Tyler.

The Scleroderma Foundation

Persons interested in scleroderma can obtain the latest information on this illness and its treatment by contacting the Scleroderma Foundation. The foundation provides up-to-date information on what scientists might have discovered about the nature of this illness and on what changes, if any, have taken place in treatment. The foundation can be contacted at (800) 722-4673. Its Web site is www.scleroderma.org .

Culture House Books

Culture House Books is a small company that publishes books about sports and show business personalities. For more information on Culture House Books, you can call 641-791-3072, or write to Culture House Books, P.O. Box 293, Newton, Iowa 50208.

About the Authors

Mike Chapman

After working for 35 years as a newspaper writer, editor and publisher, Mike Chapman retired in 2002 to work fulltime as the executive director of the International Wrestling Institute and Museum in Newton, Iowa. He and his wife, Bev, founded the museum in 1997.

Much of Mr. Chapman's life has been spent in the world of wrestling. He has been named National Wrestling Writer of the Year four times, created W.I.N. magazine, the nation's leading publication on amateur wrestling, and has won numerous awards in the sport.

A lifelong fan of B western films, Mr. Chapman is also well-known in Tarzan circles. He has hosted two national Tarzan conventions (known as dum dums) and in 2004 was presented "The Golden Lion Award" for lifetime achievement in preserving the heritage of Tarzan.

The Tom Tyler Story is his 17th book. Other recent books by Mr. Chapman are *Achilles: Son of Peleus, Scourge of Troy,* and *Lowell Park,* both historical novels. He has also written the biographies of two movie Tarzans – *Please Don't Call Me Tarzan* (the story of Herman Brix, aka Bruce Bennett), and *The Gold and The Glory* (the story of Glenn Morris, 1936 Olympic decathlon champion and World War II officer).

Mike and Bev Chapman live in Newton, Iowa and have three grown children.

Bobby Copeland

Bobby Copeland is a long-time B-western movie enthusiast. He has written some 150 articles, authored 10 books and has contributed to 15 other books about the western film performers. In addition, he has attended over 60 film festivals and met many of the actors and actresses who participated in these grand old films. He has studied the genre for over 25 years and is routinely called upon to answer questions regarding the old Saturday matinee cowboys.

Bobby resides in Oak Ridge, Tennessee (near Knoxville) with his wife Joan, who shares his interest in B-western films.